# Lost and Found

## the art of David Brady

David Brady is a Los Angeles artist known for his continuous exploration of the figure through mixed media and his use of found objects. Utilizing a host of recycled materials and mediums, his collage based paintings portray powerful and provocative images that reflect contemporary life. His creations include collage, assemblage, oil, and drawing as well as digitally based works and publications.

His appetite for everything creative has landed him an artist residency in Japan, collaborative projects with Nelson Mandela, poet Amde Hamilton, photo-journalist David Butow, and composer Mark Sims.

Exhibitions and projects include the Museum of Fine Art Cuba, Modern Art Museum Mexico, Turchin Center for the Arts, The Lincoln Center, Lilia Arts Center, MOCA Los Angeles, World Trade Center Osaka, Hammer Museum, and the Center for the Study of Collage. Brady's work is on exhibit at a number of galleries and universities through-out the United States and selected public spaces internationally.

For more information visit the artist online at:
www.bradyart.com

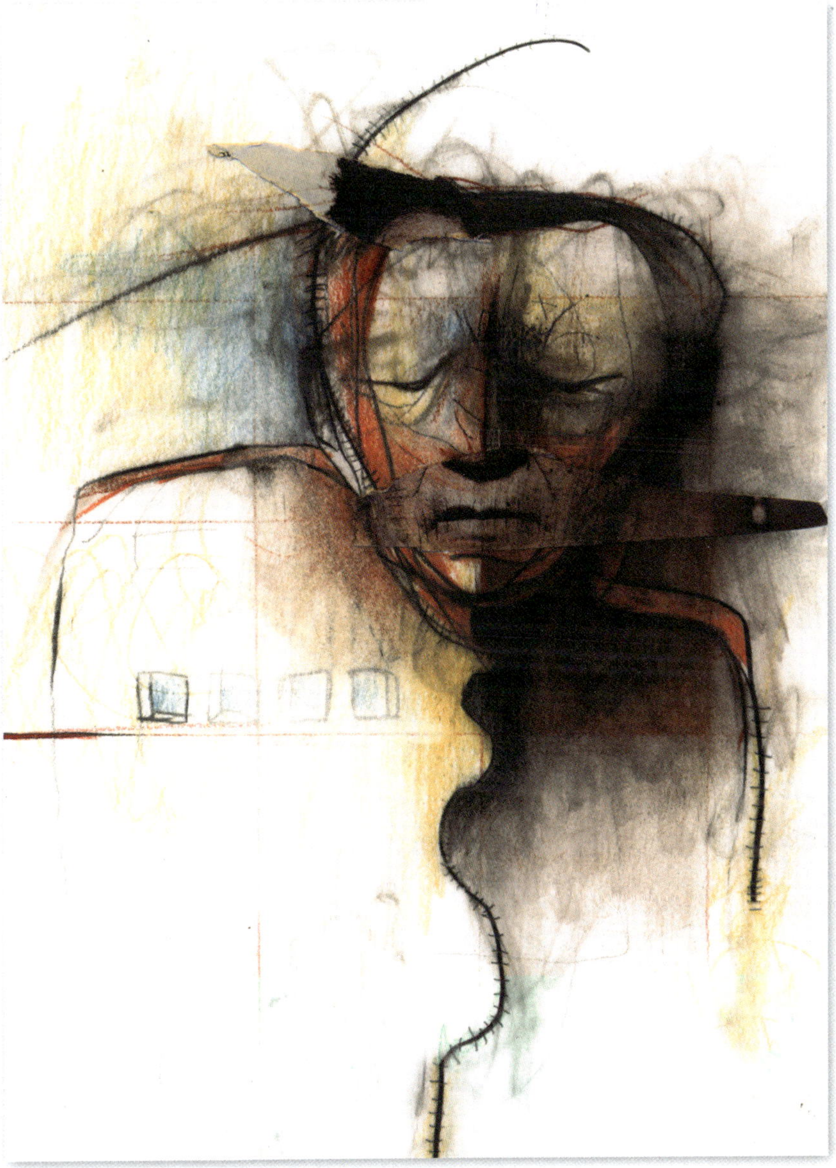

"Contemplation" • Collage with colored pencil on paper • 18"x 24" • 2006

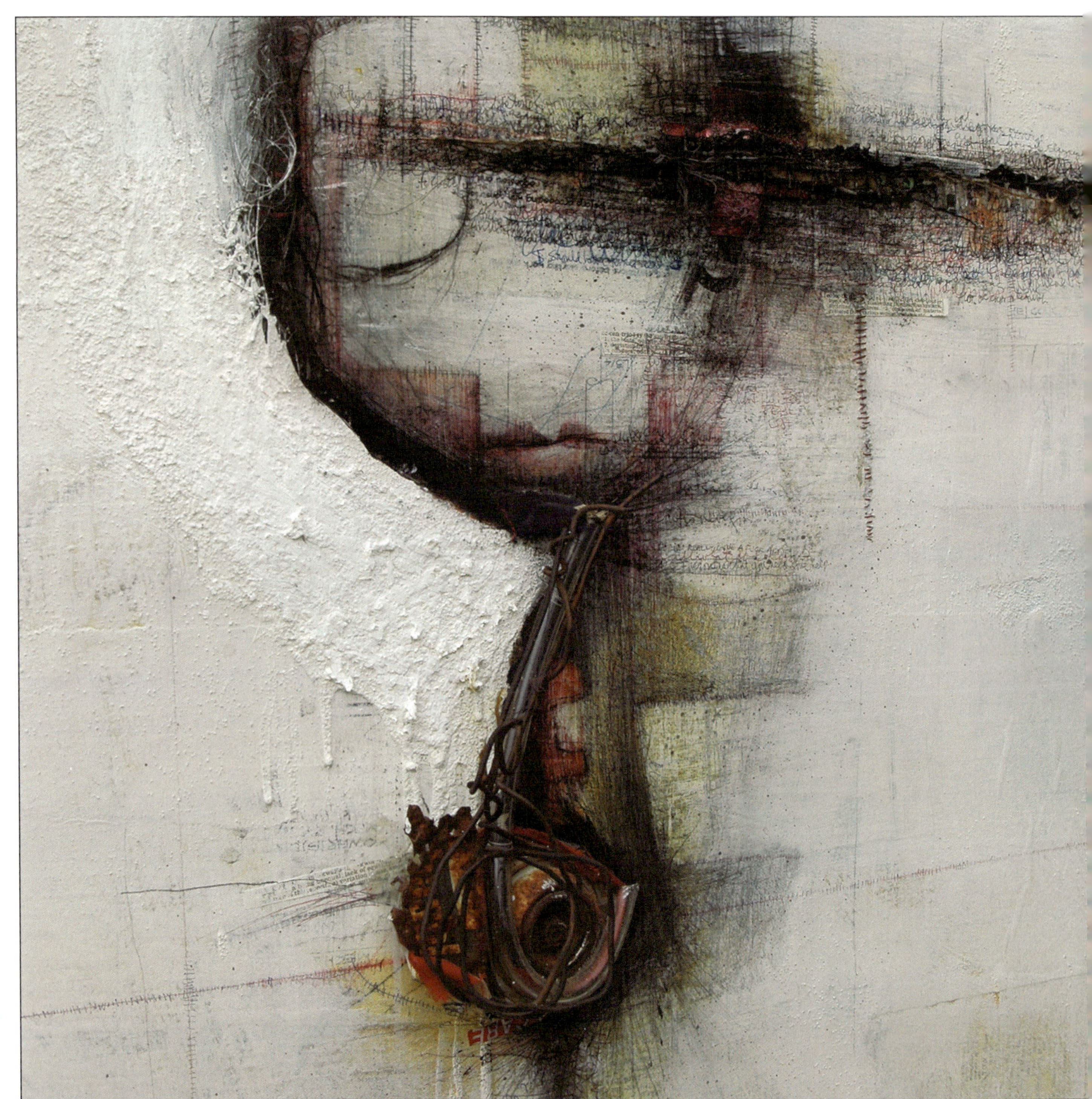

**"Left Turn"** (detail view)

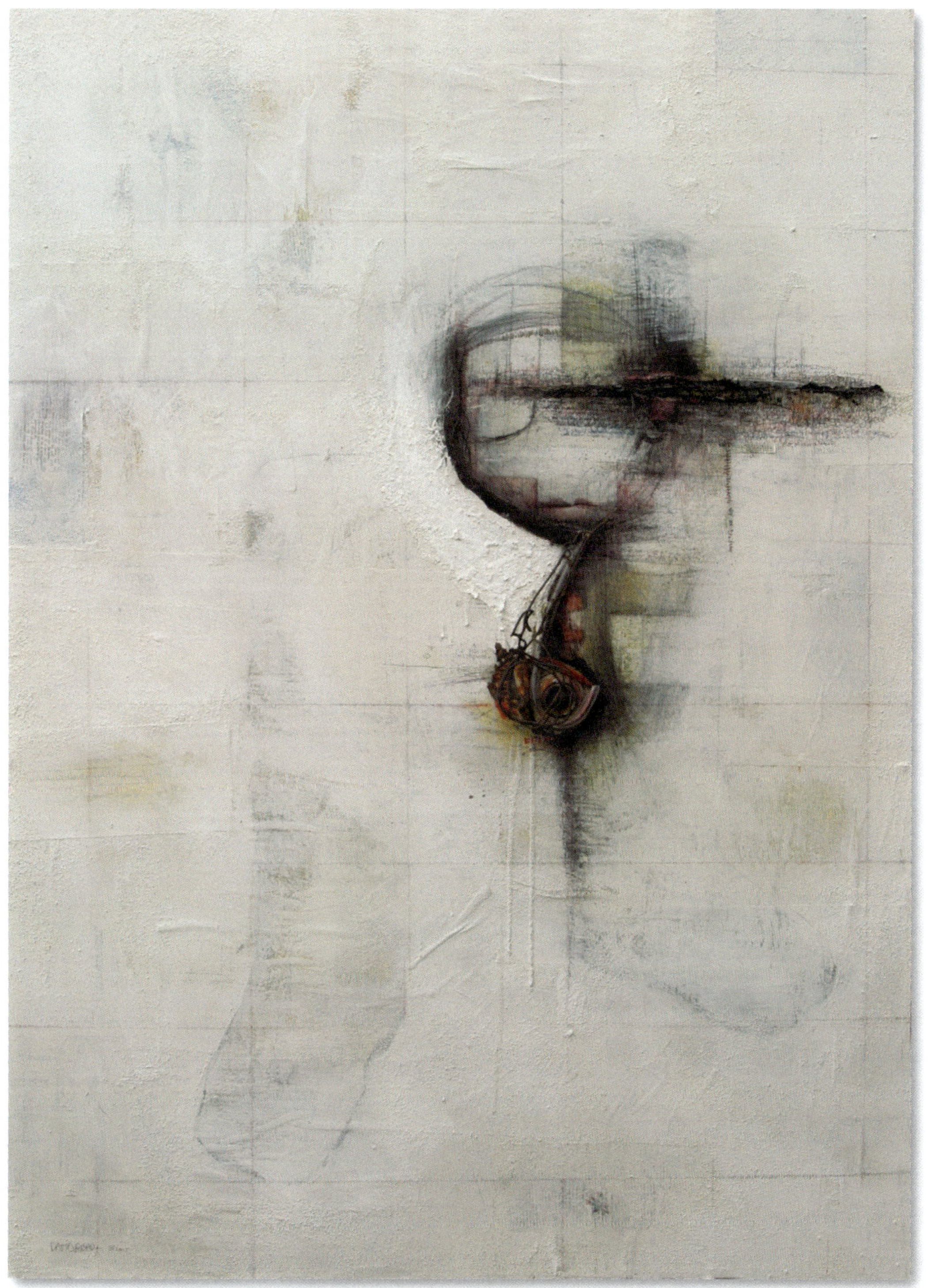

"**Left Turn**" • Oil, enamel, ballpoint pen and paper with found objects on canvas • 36"x48" • 2005

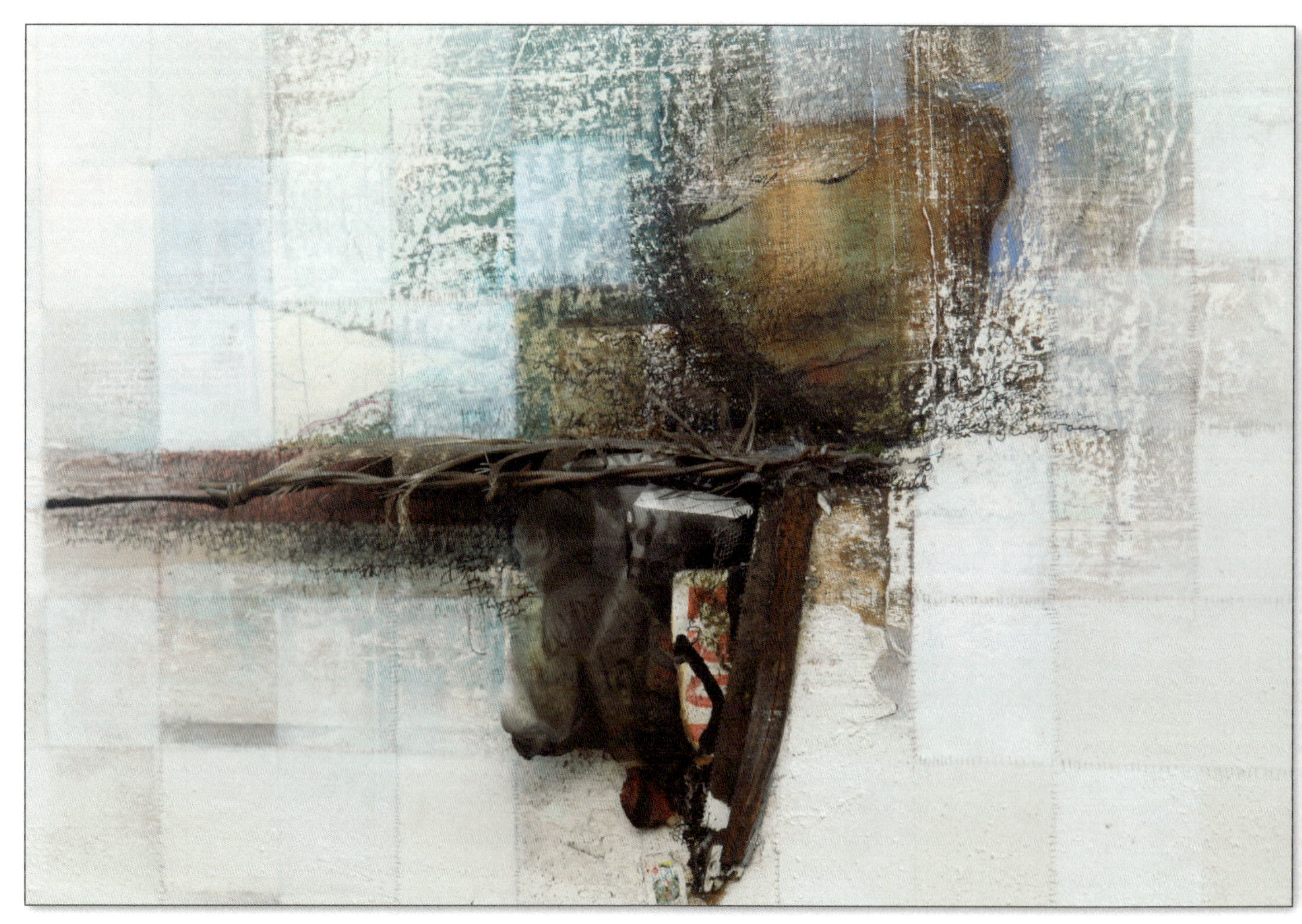

"**Little Wing**" • Oil, enamel, ballpoint pen and paper with found objects on canvas • 17"x 31" • 2007

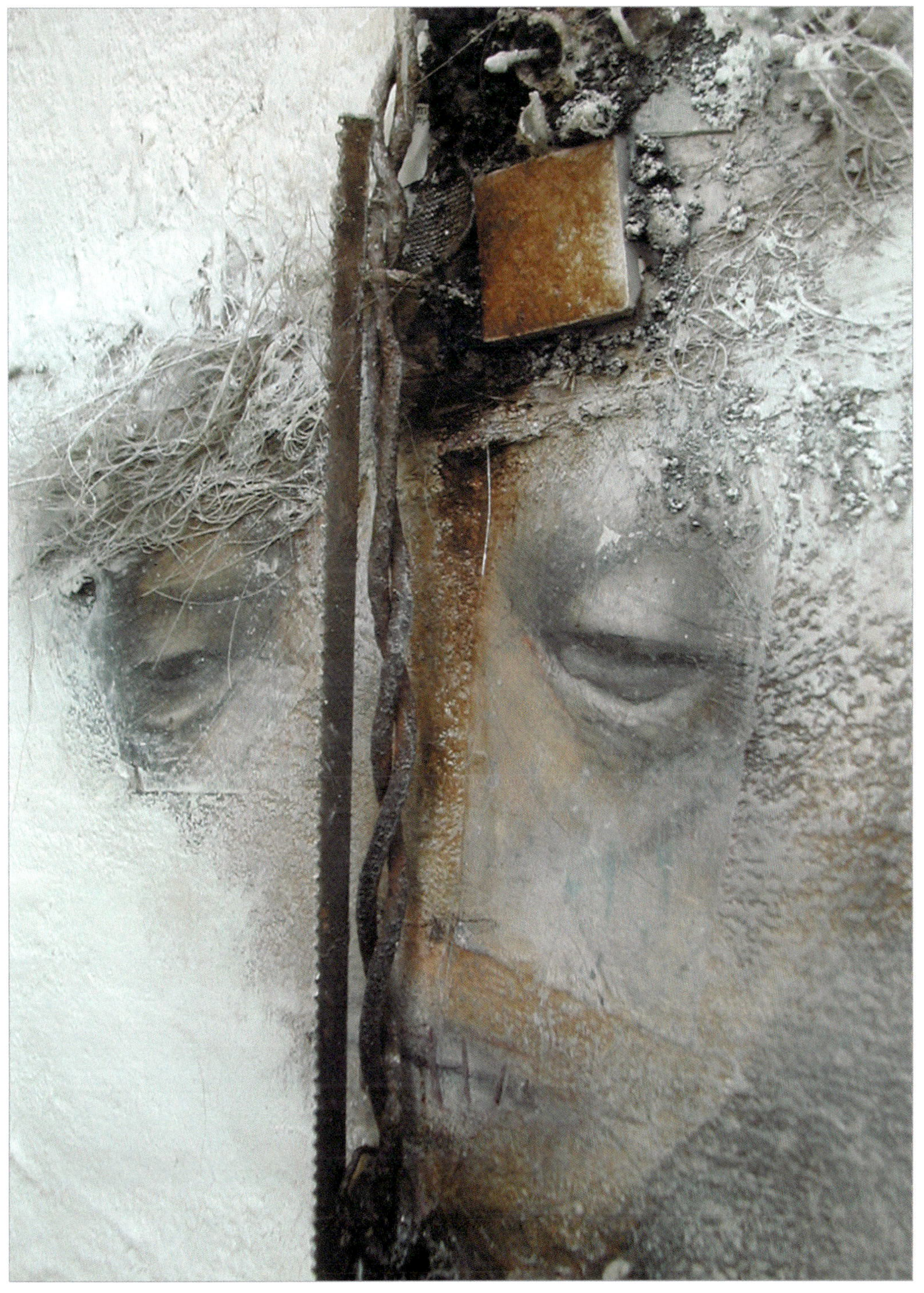

**"Peace in the Valley"** (detail view) • Oil, enamel, thread and paper with found objects on canvas • 36"x 48" • 2005

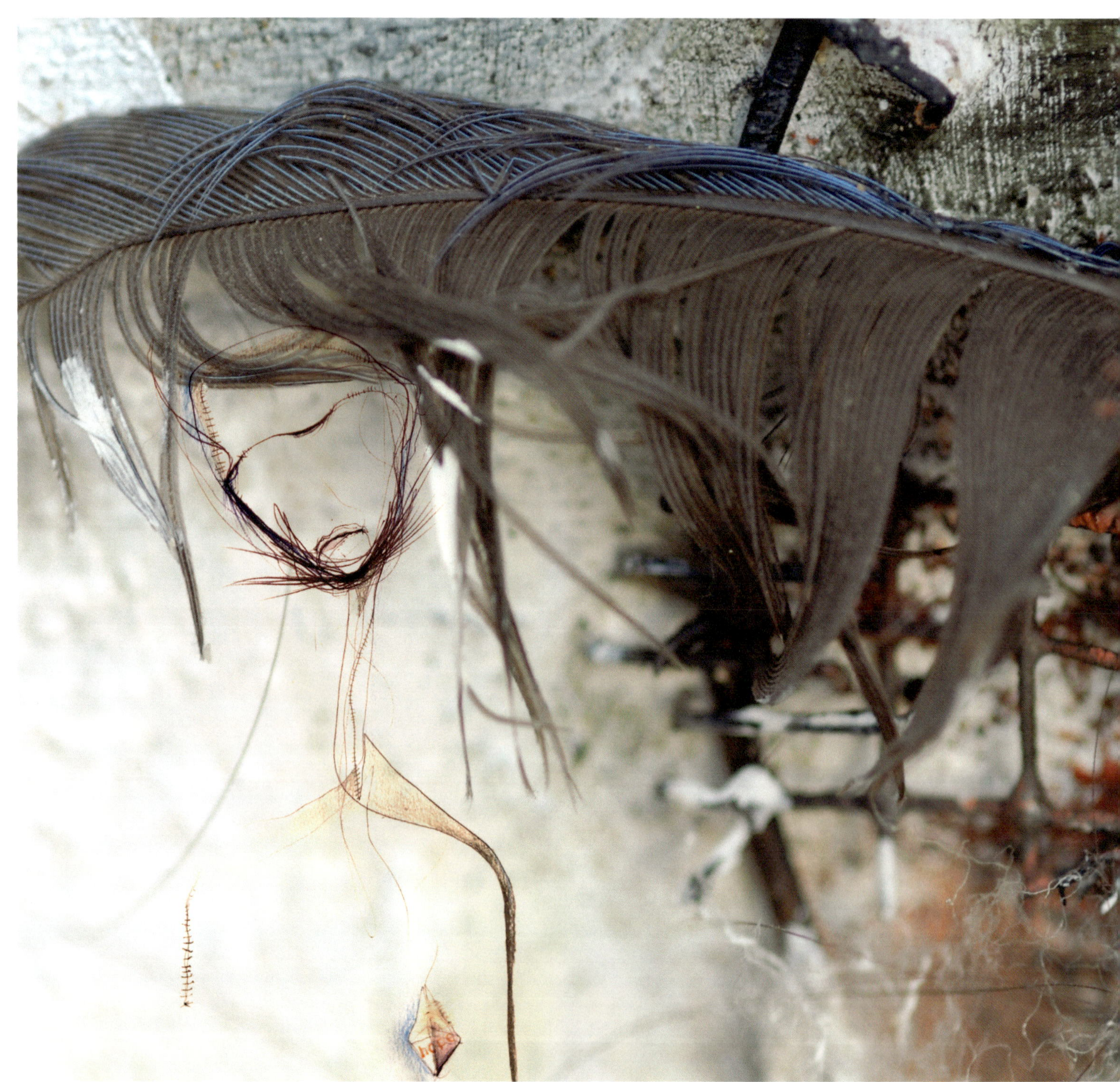

"**Fragile Shelter**" • Digital collage on watercolor paper • 12"x 14" • 2010

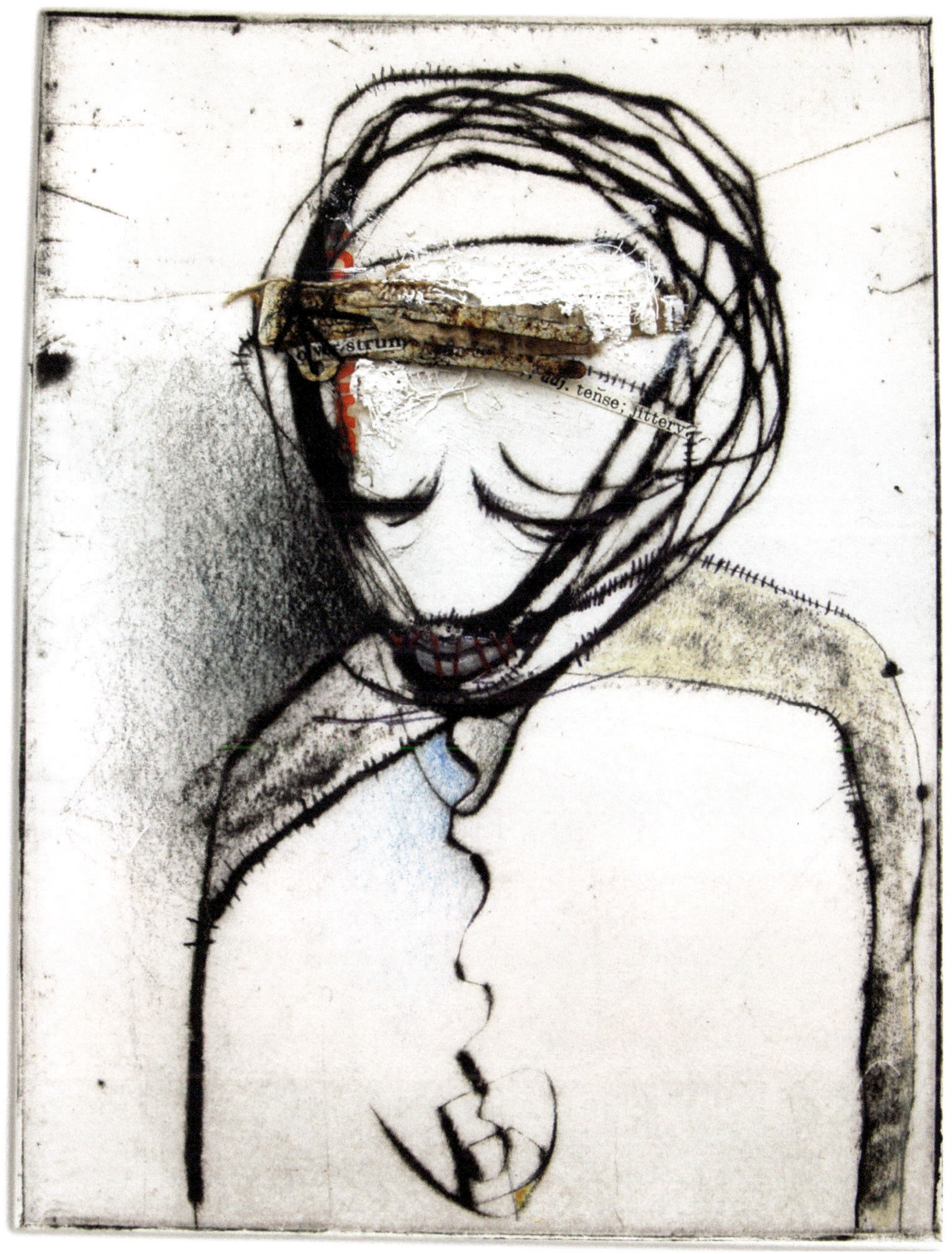

**"Don't Speak"** • Etching and collage with found objects and thread on paper • 5"x 7" • 2005

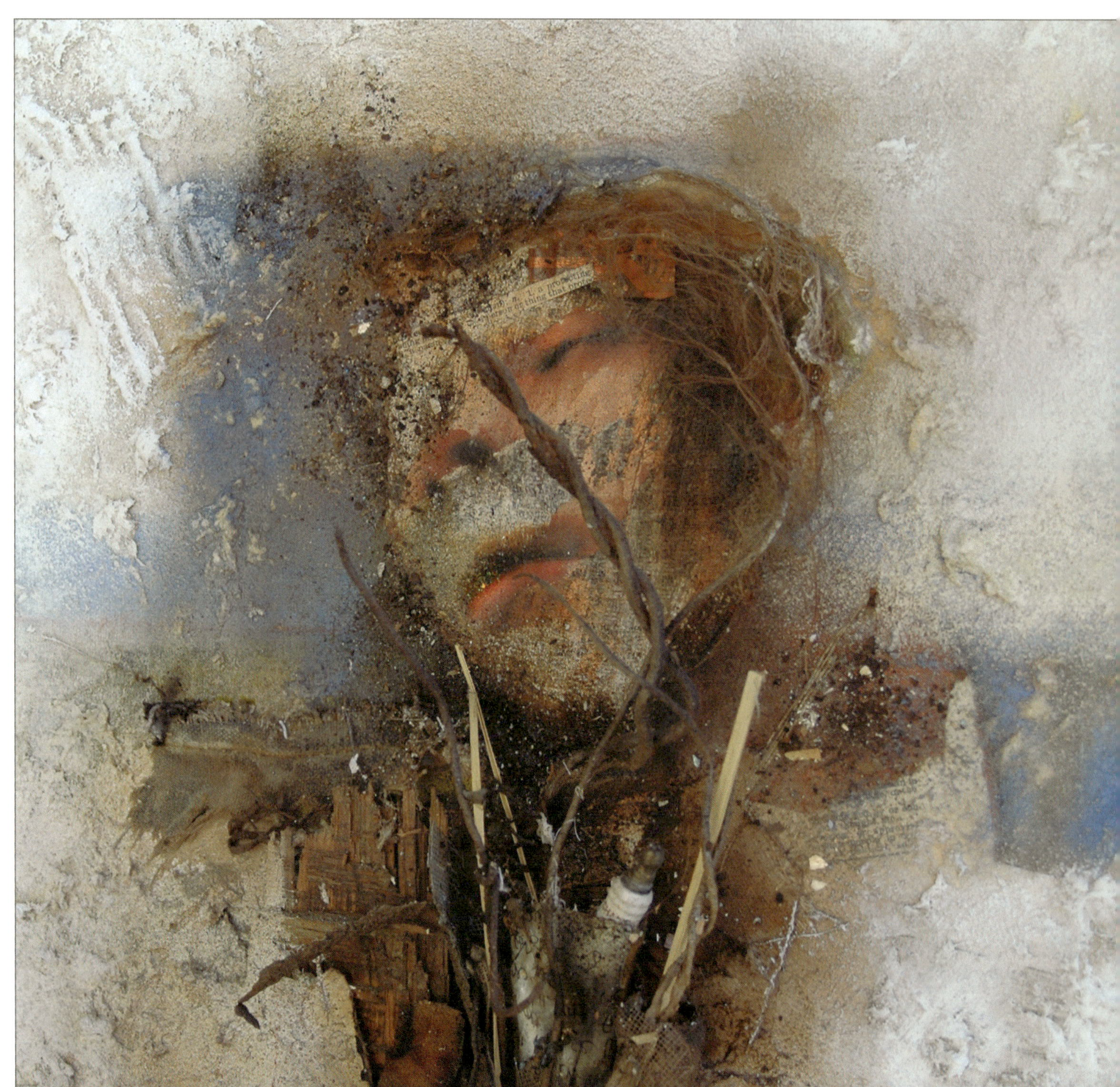

"**Addiction**" (detail view)

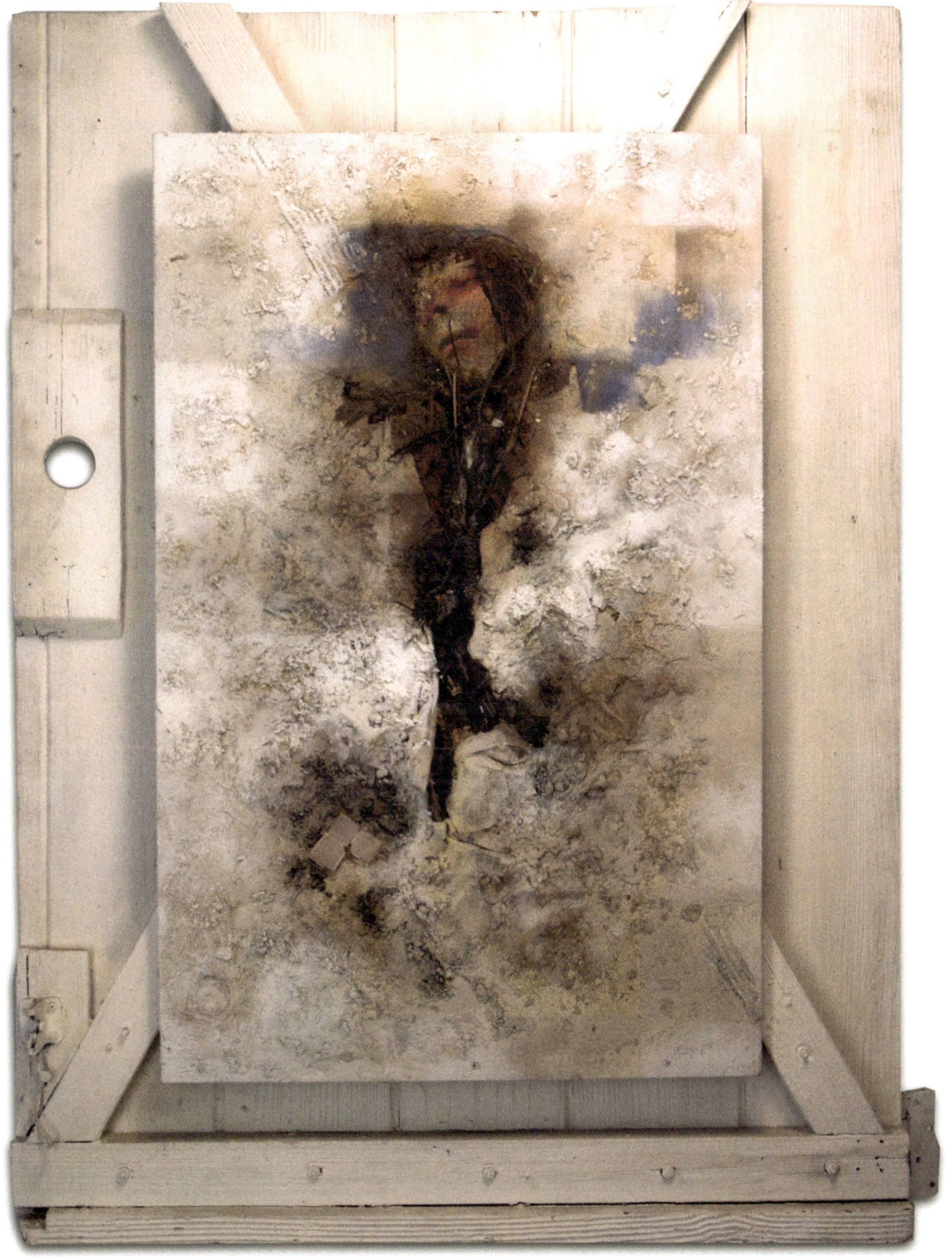

"**Addiction**" • Oil and mixed media with found objects and fabric on canvas and wood gate • 37″ x 48″ • 2005

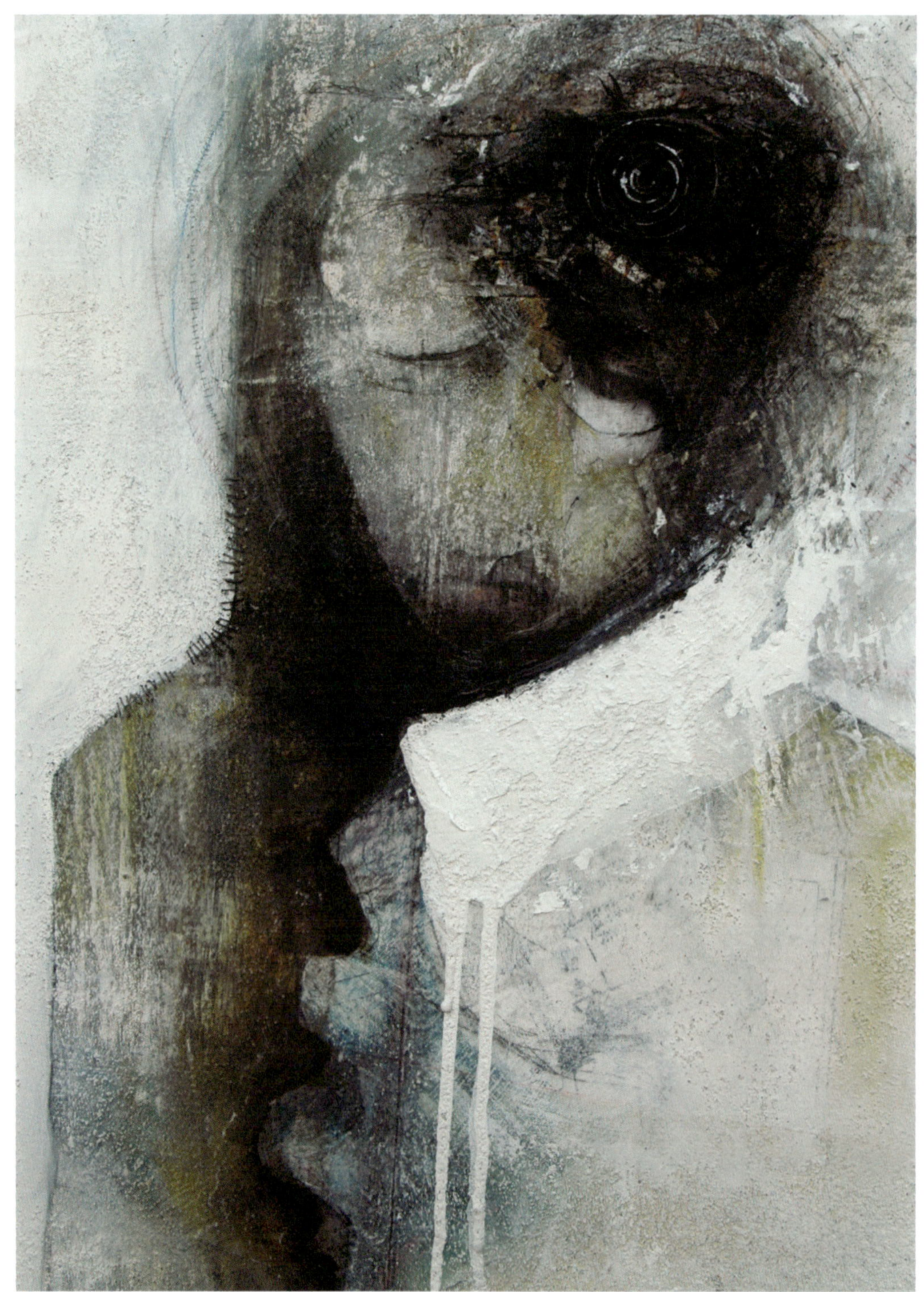

"**Spinning**" (detail view)

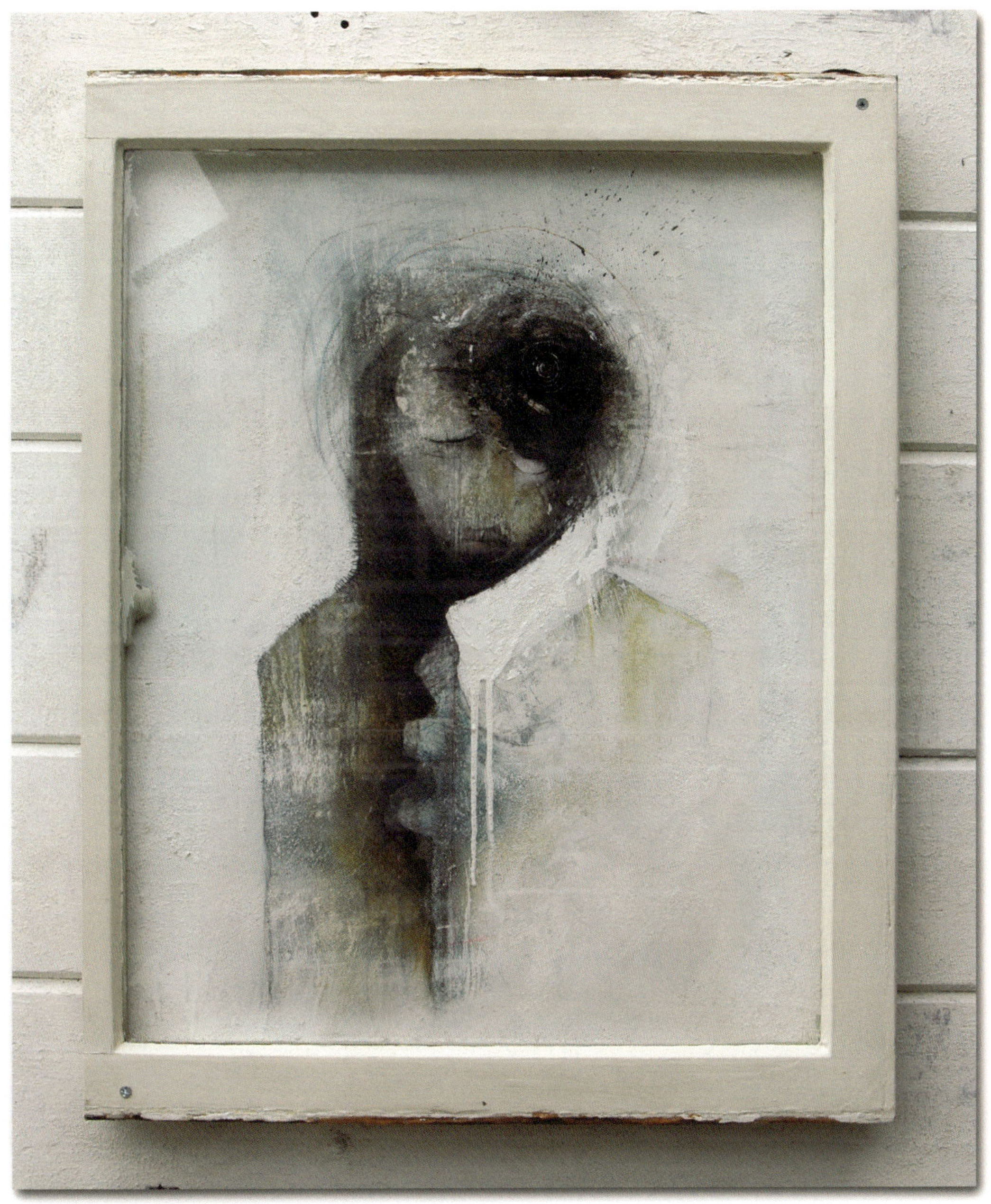

"**Spinning**" • Oil, enamel, ballpoint pen, thread and paper with found objects on canvas in window frame • 30″ x 36″ • 2007

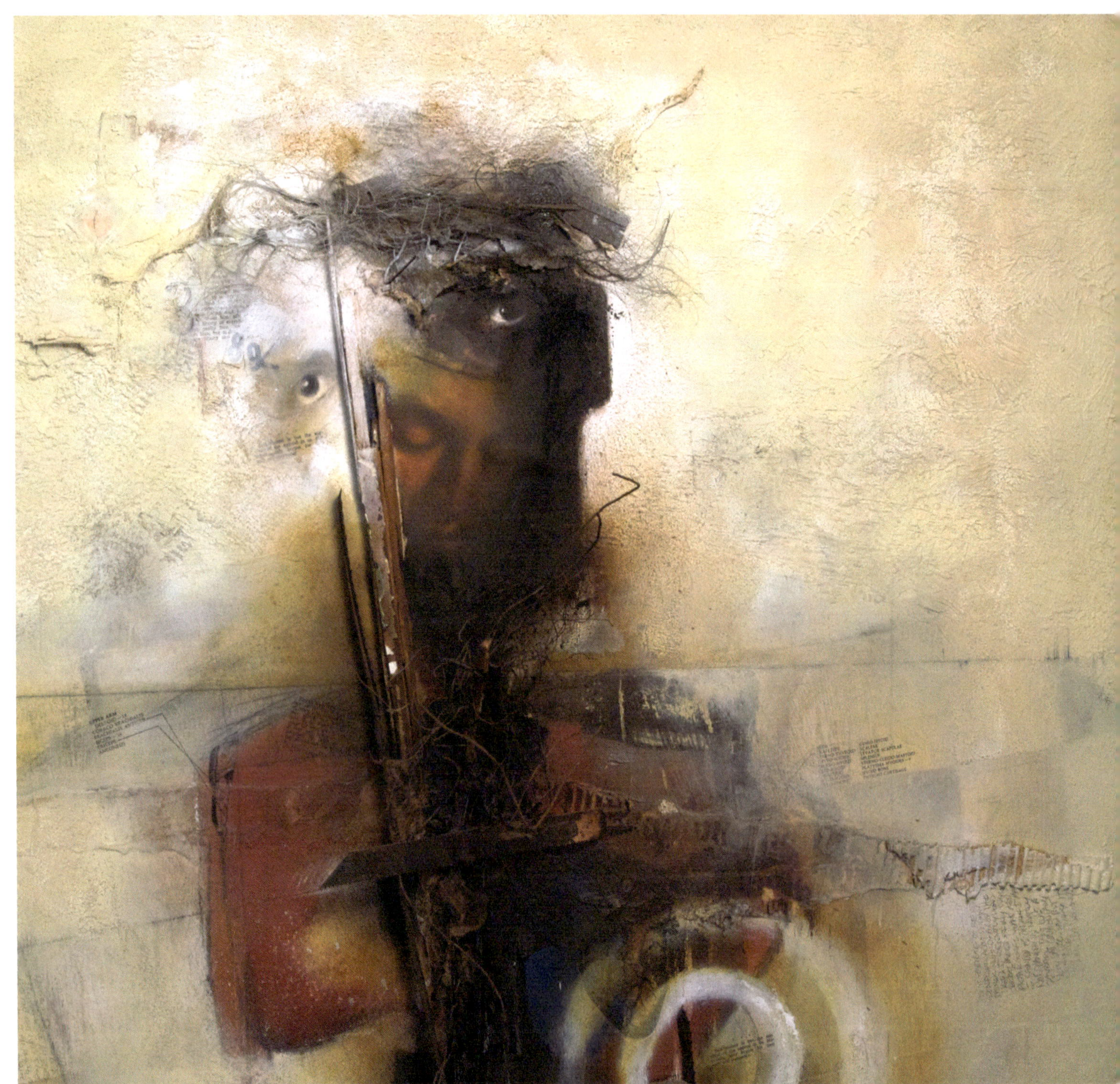

**"Shielded"** (detail view)

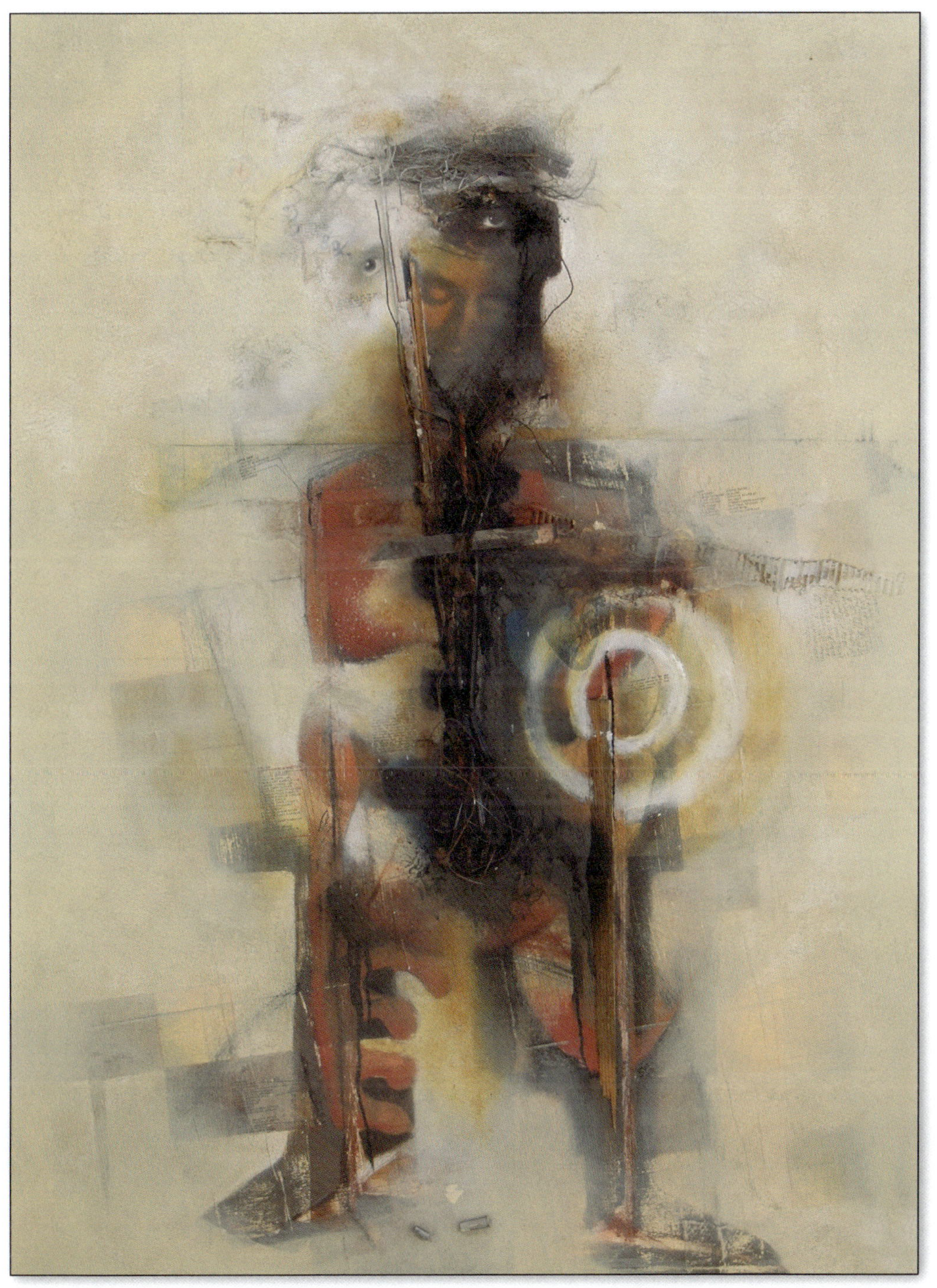

"**Shielded**" • Oil, enamel and paper with found objects on canvas • 36"x48" • 2002

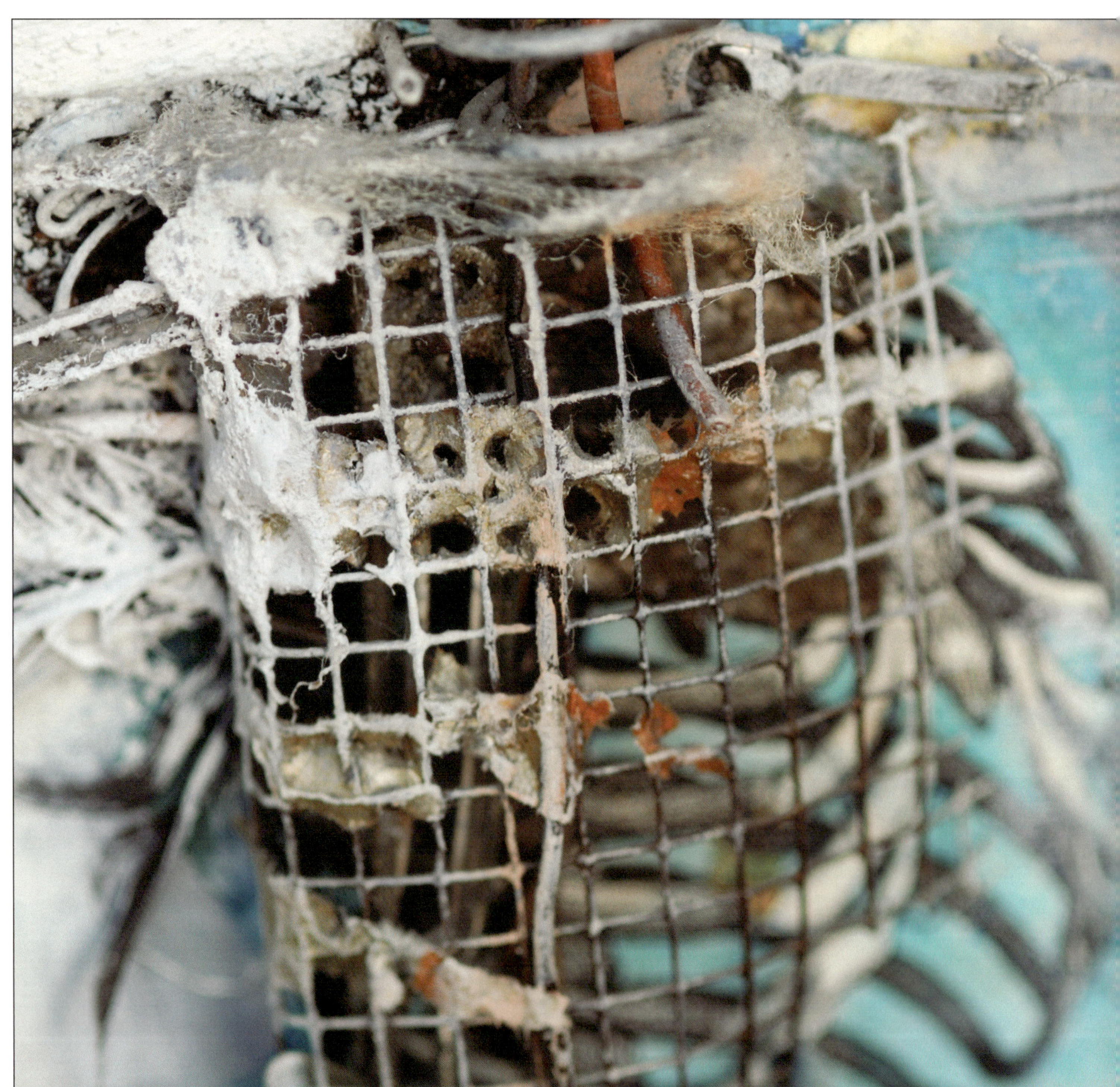

**"Remains"** (detail view)

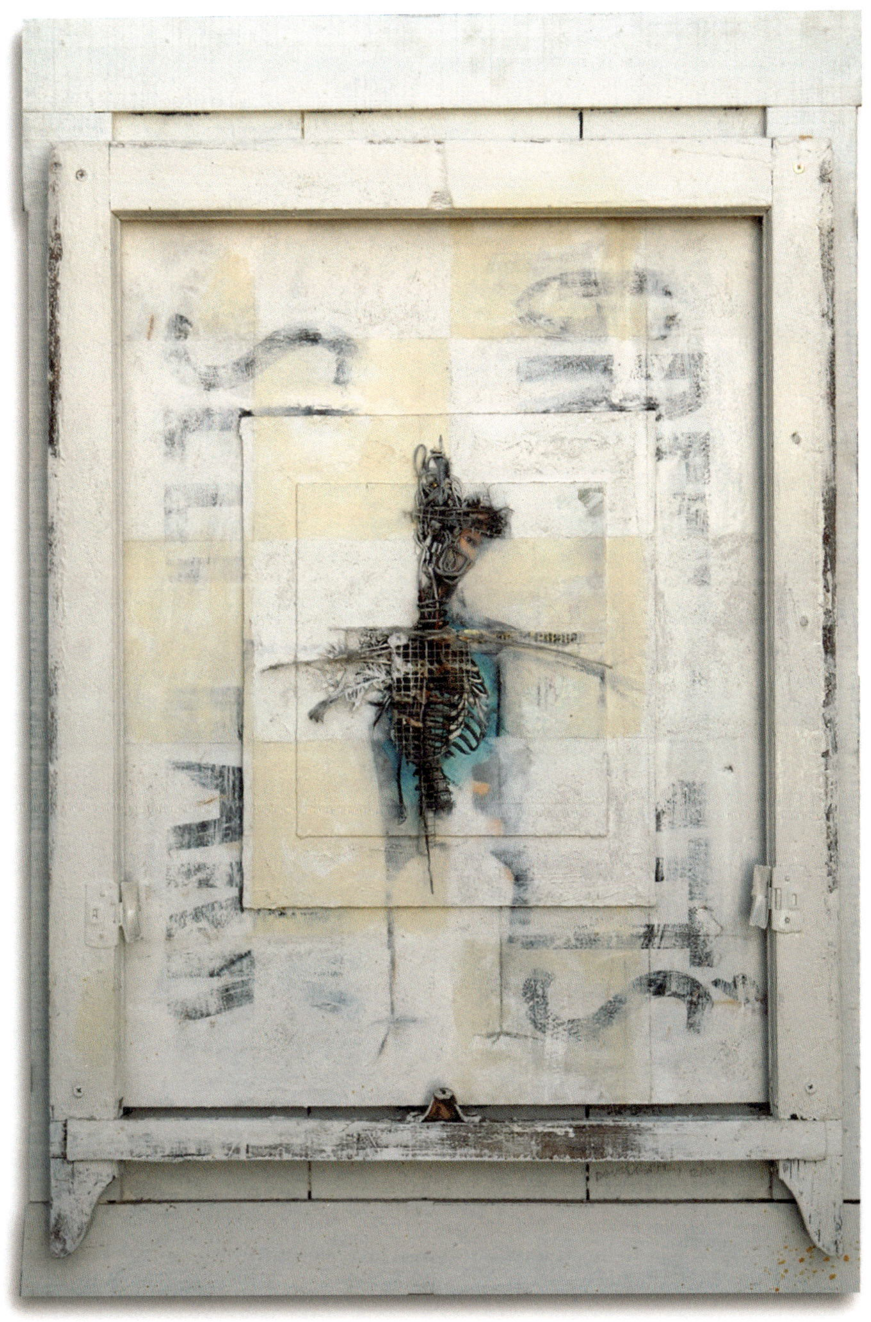

"**Remains**" • Oil, enamel with found objects on metal sign and wood • 24"x 38" • 2002

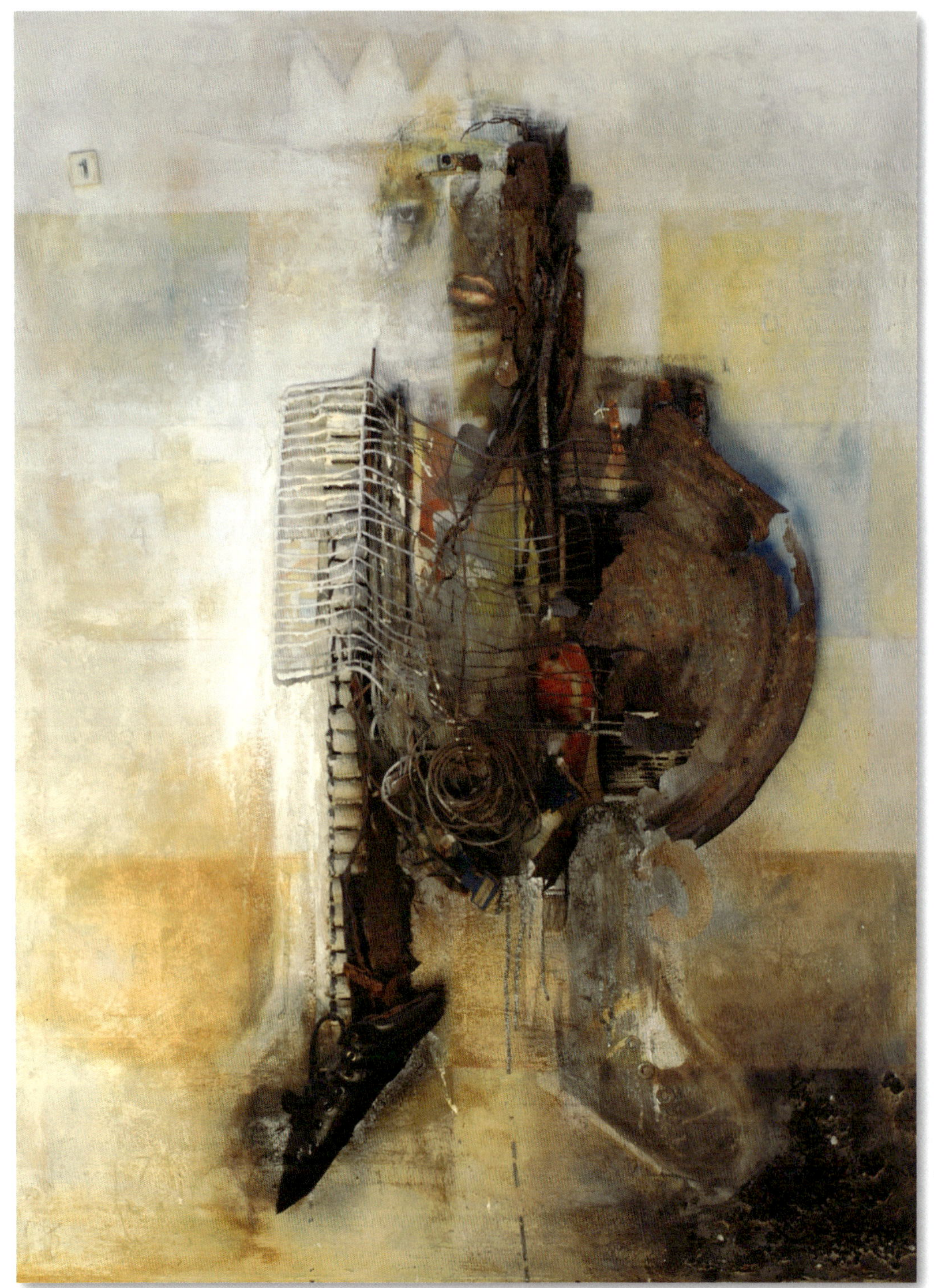


"**The Quest**" • Oil, enamel, paper with found objects on canvas • 36"x48" • 2005

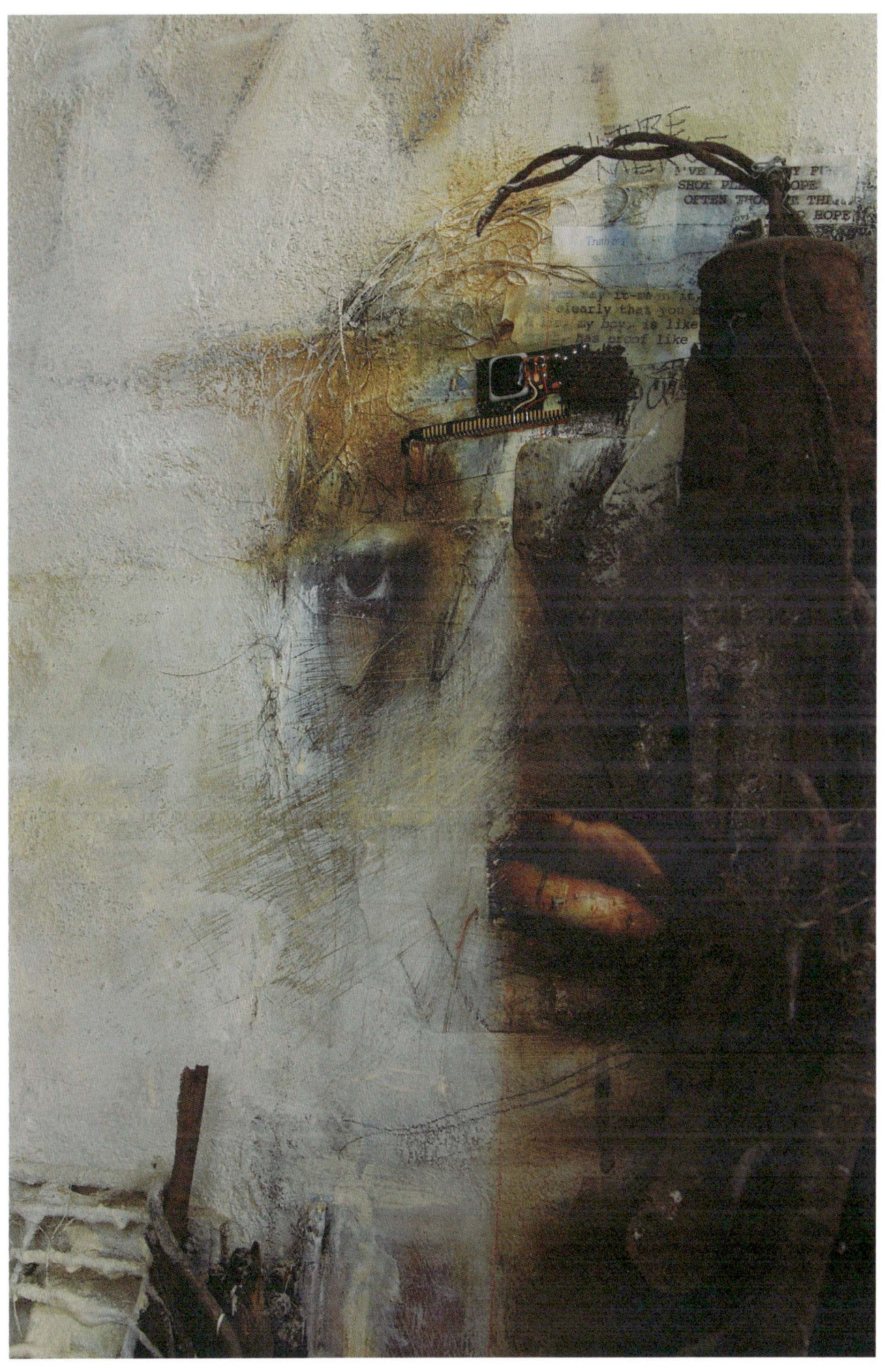

**"The Quest"** (detail view)

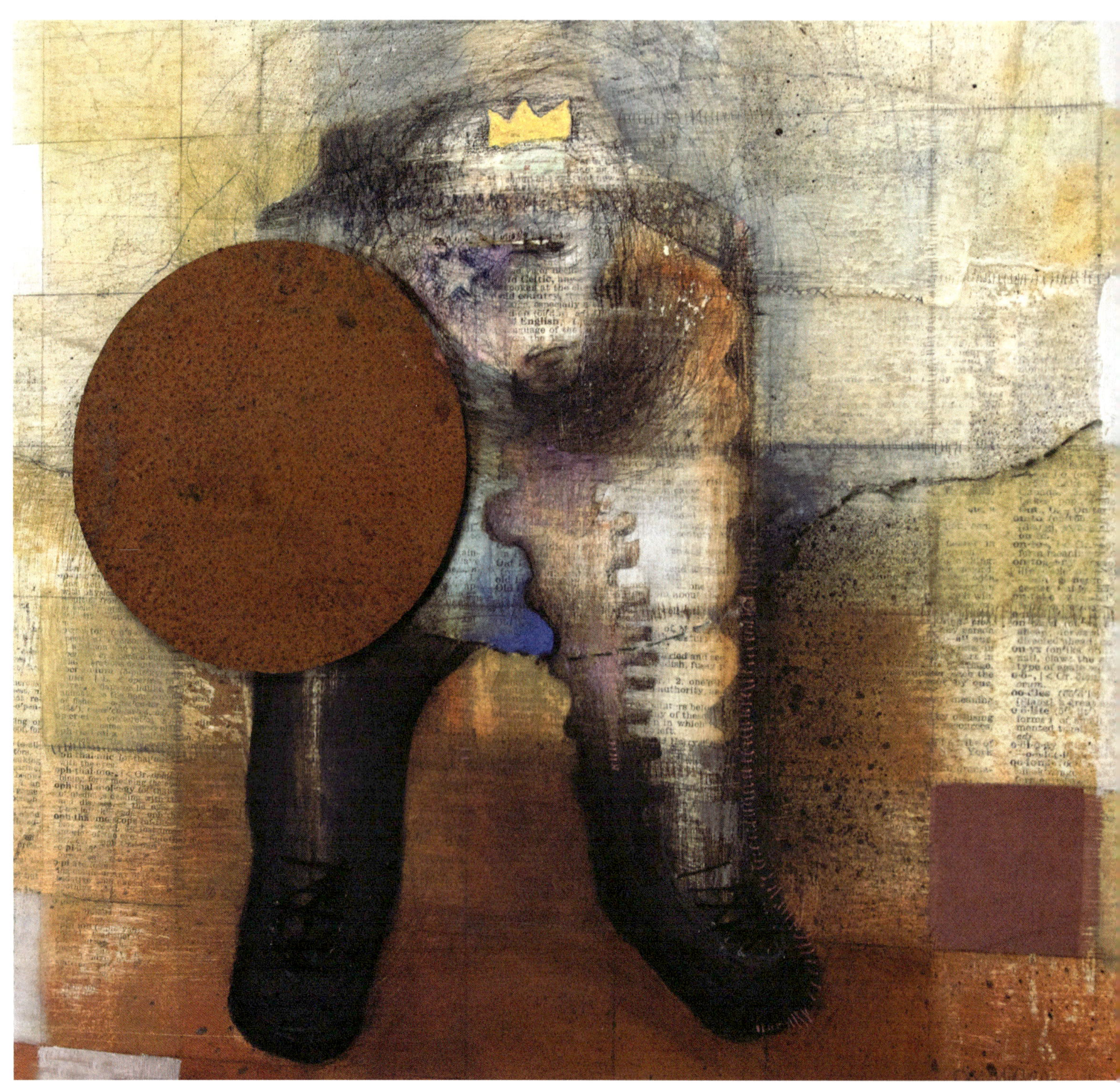

"**The American**" (detail view) • Oil, sand, ballpoint pen and paper with found objects on canvas • 16"x25" • 2005

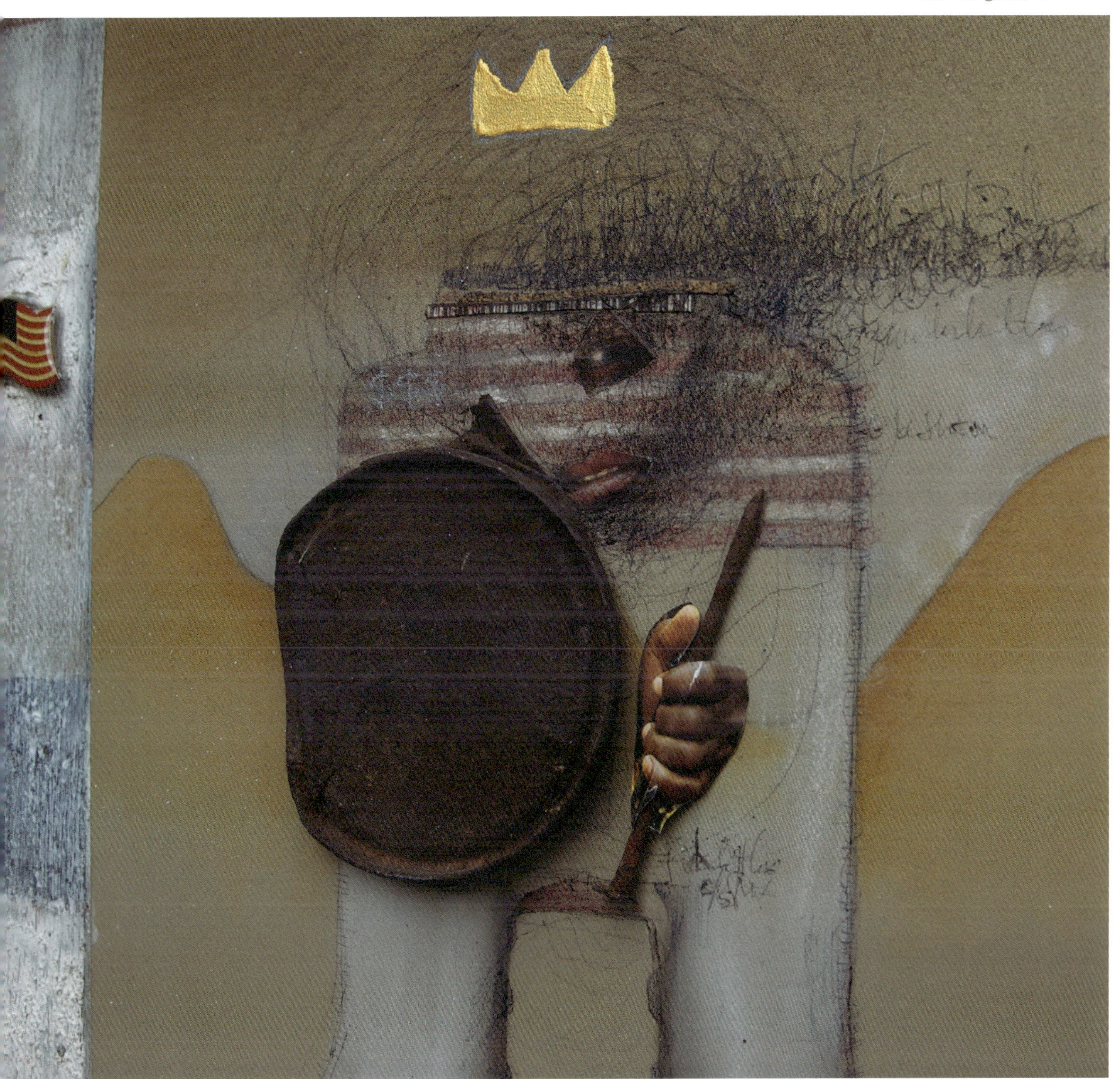

"**History Box**" (detail view) • Oil, ballpoint pen and collage with found objects on wood box • 25"x 24" • 2007

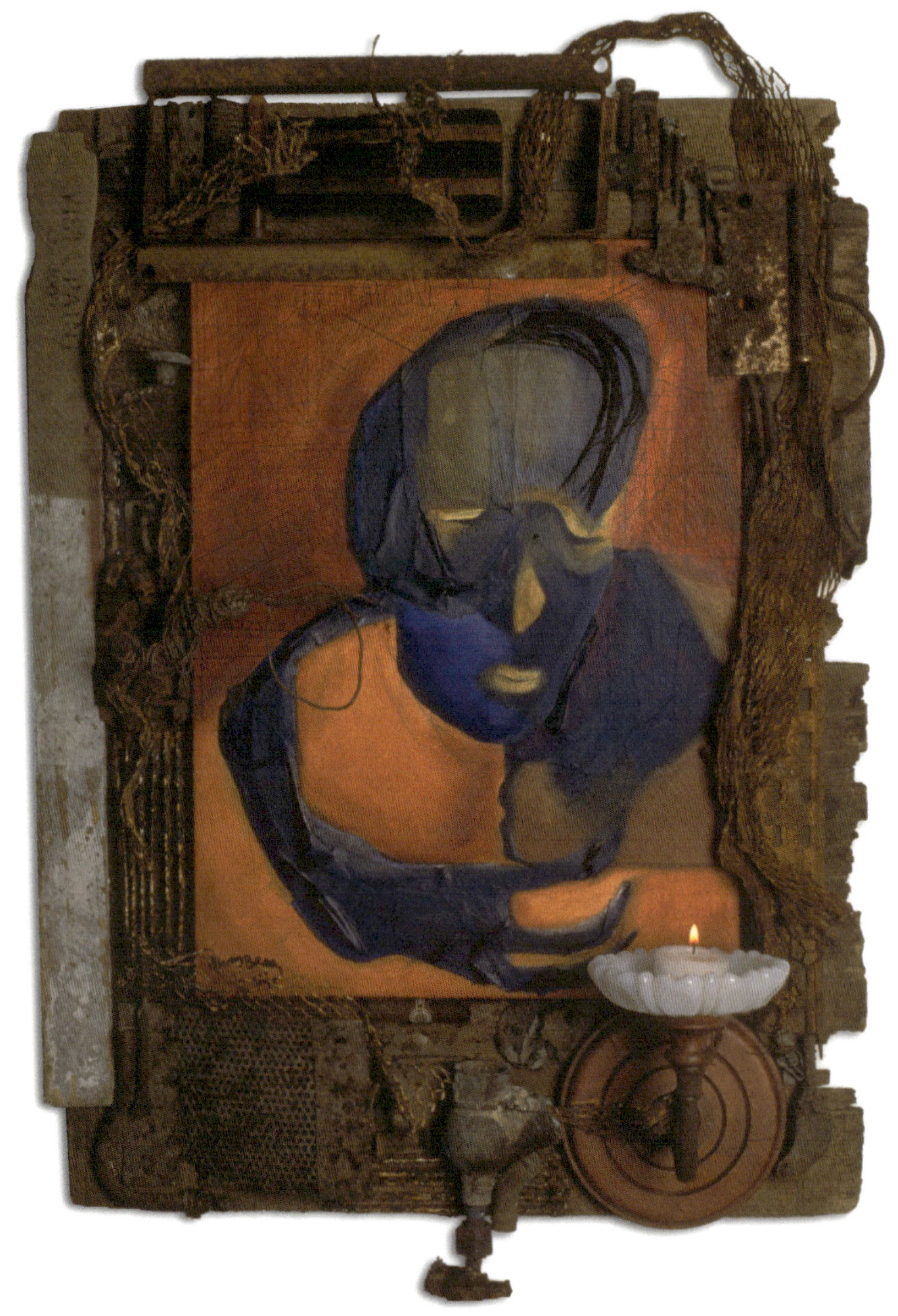

"**Lost and Found**" • Oil and paper with found objects on canvas and wood • 22"x 38" • 1998

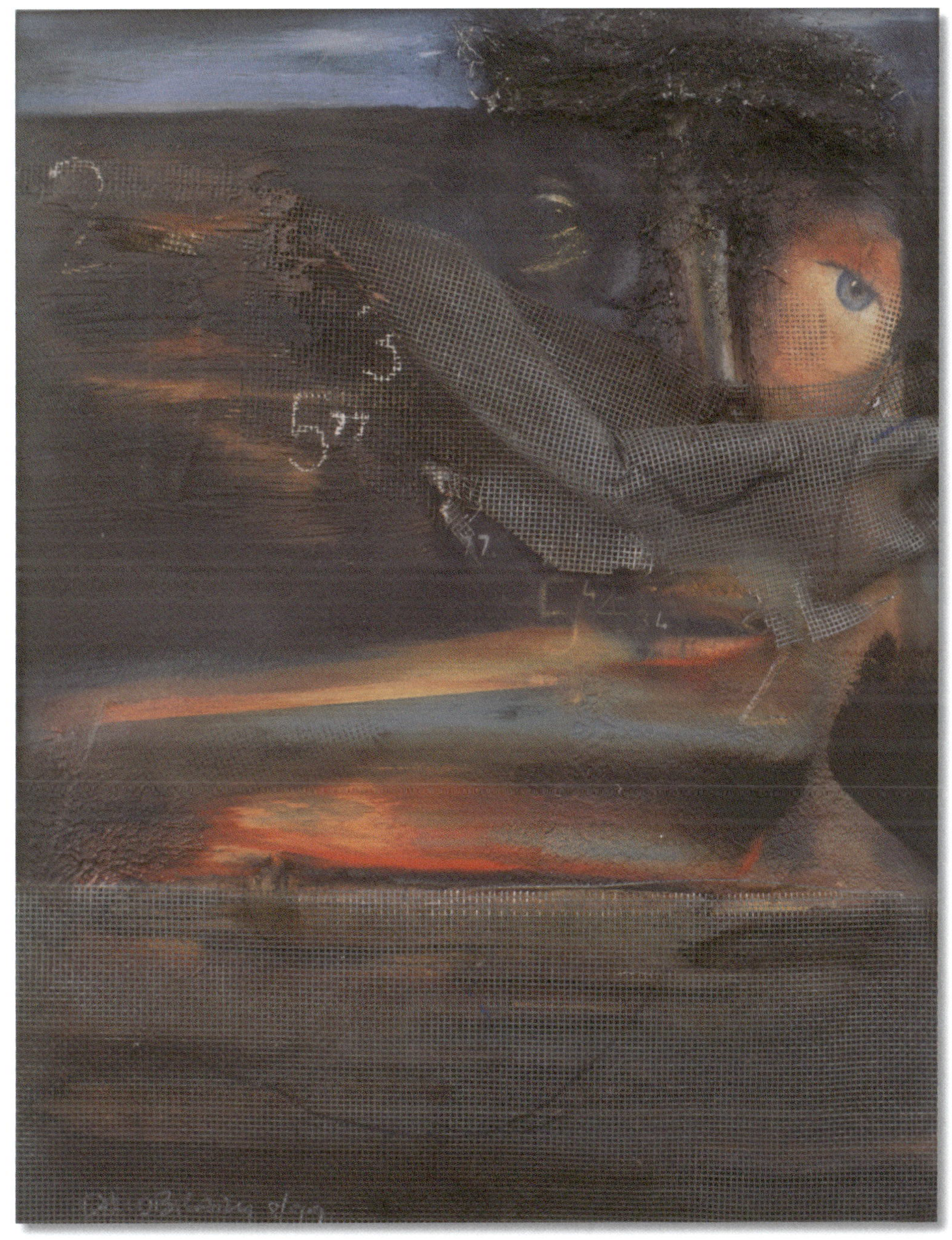

**"Surfaces"** • Oil, collage and wire on board • 10"x 12" • 1999

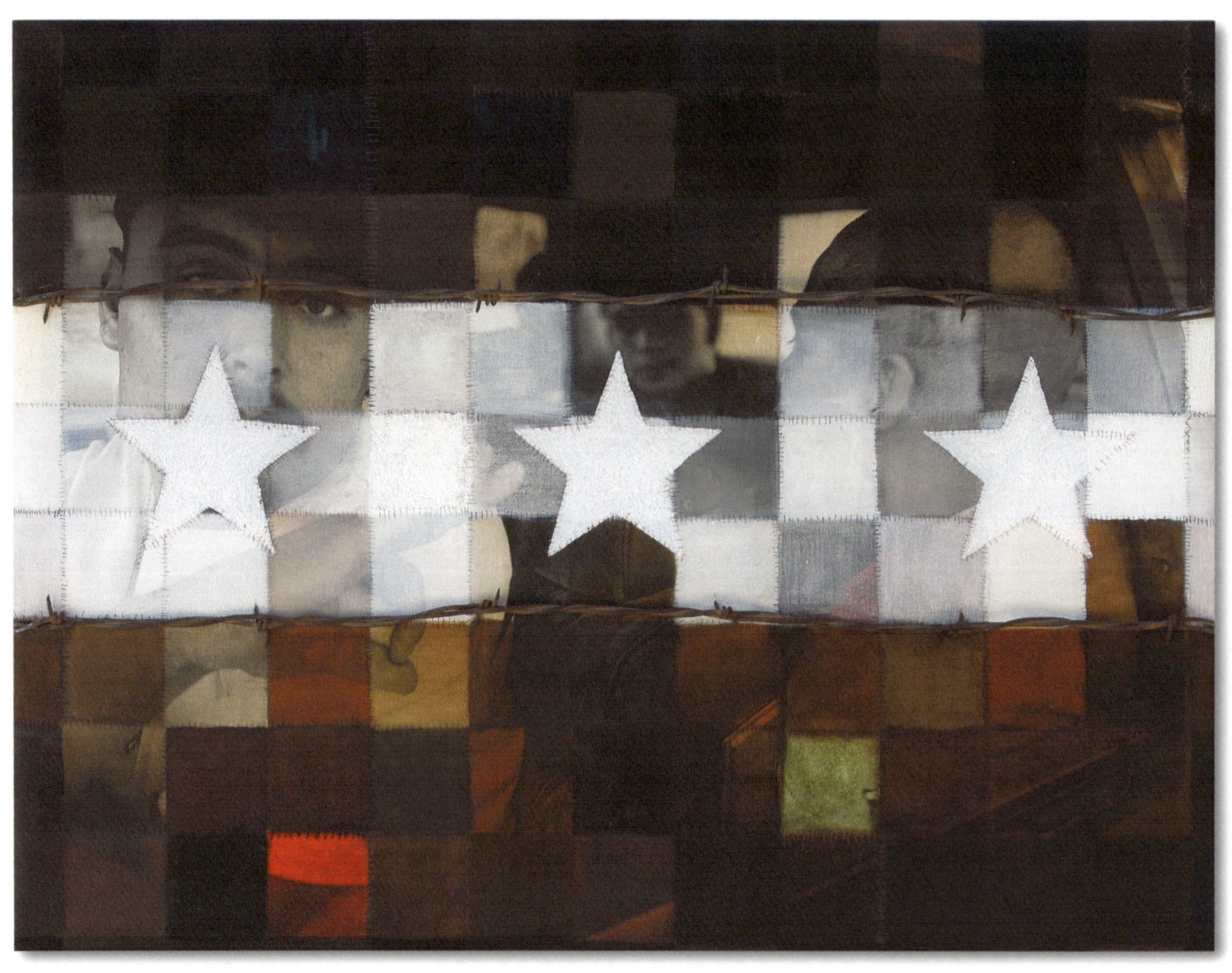

"**Flag 5, Study for Assimilation**" • Oil, ballpoint pen and barbwire on canvas print • 19.5"x 25.5" • 2007

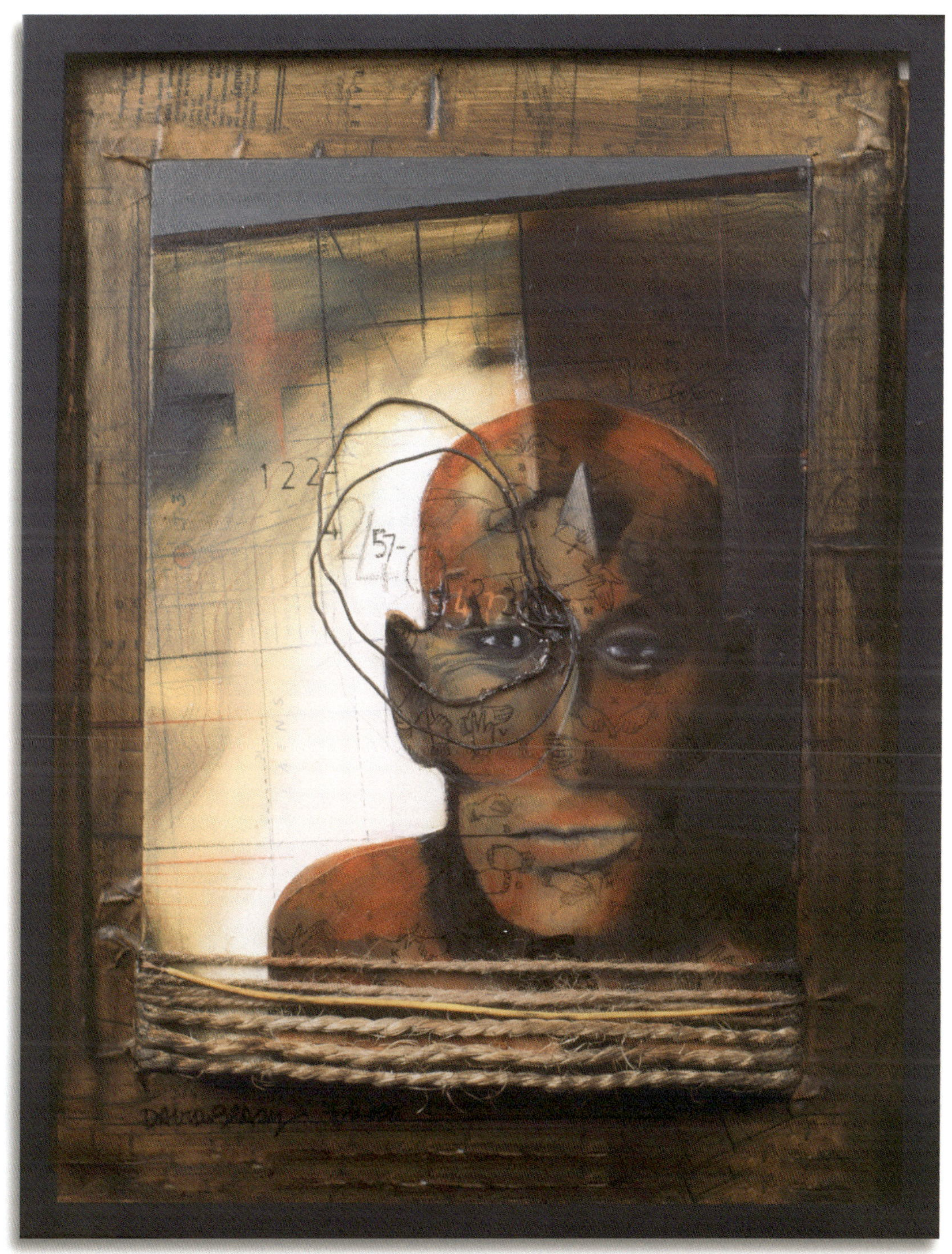

**"Hand Signals"** • Oil, paper, rope and wire on canvas • 12"x16" • 2005

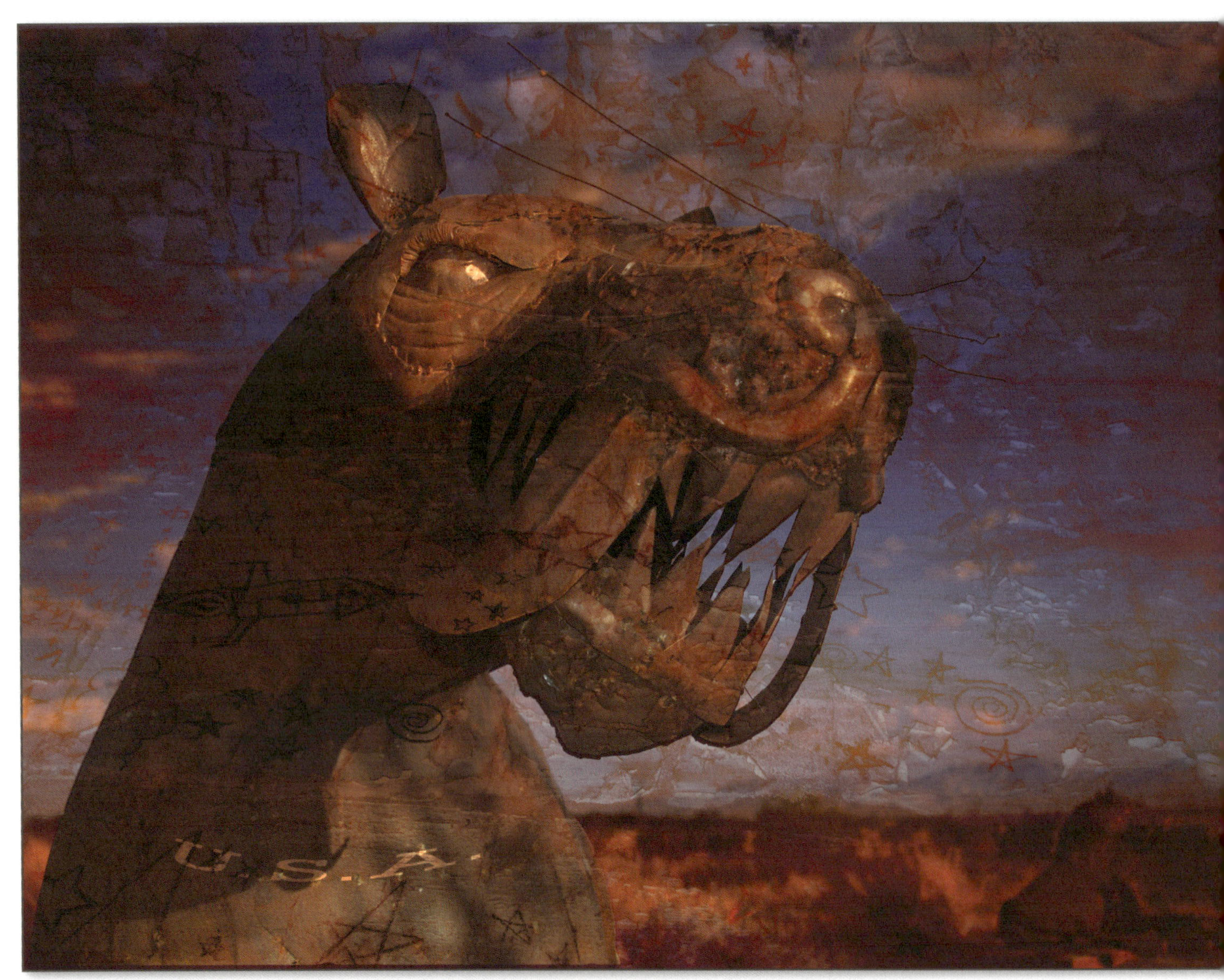

**"American Greed"** • Digital collage, pigment print on watercolor paper • 13"x 17" • 2010

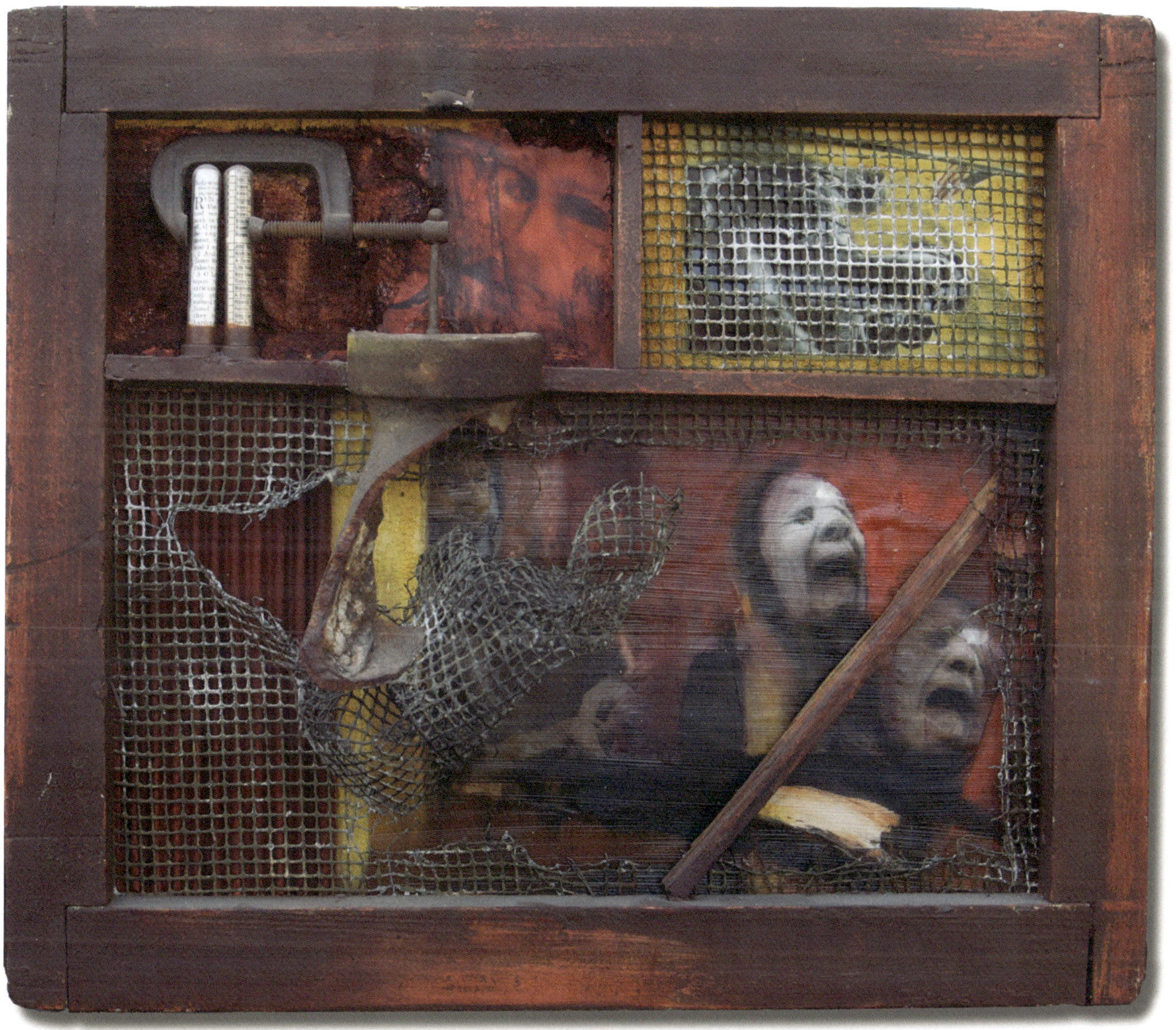

"**Defending our Beliefs**" • Oil, photographs and found objects on board • 16"x19" • 1995

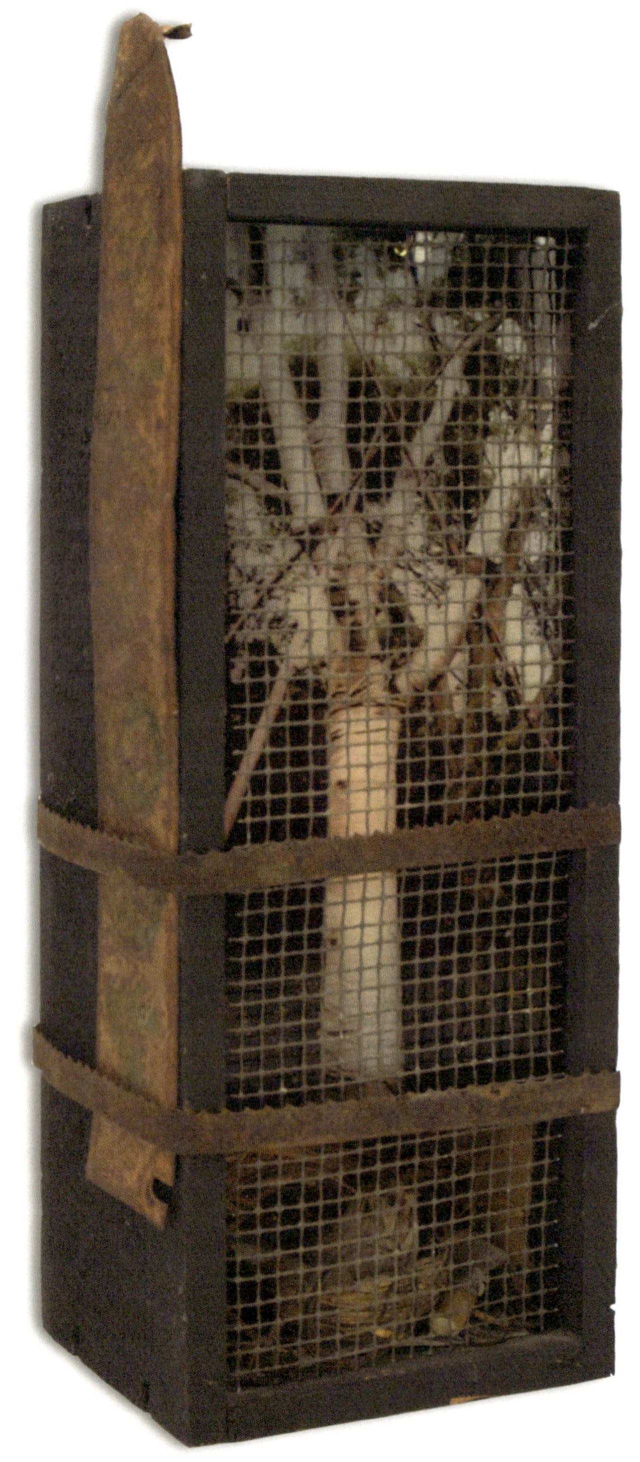

"**Bounded Box**" • Found objects with stuffed bird in wine box   • 4.5"x 5.5" 14" • 2007

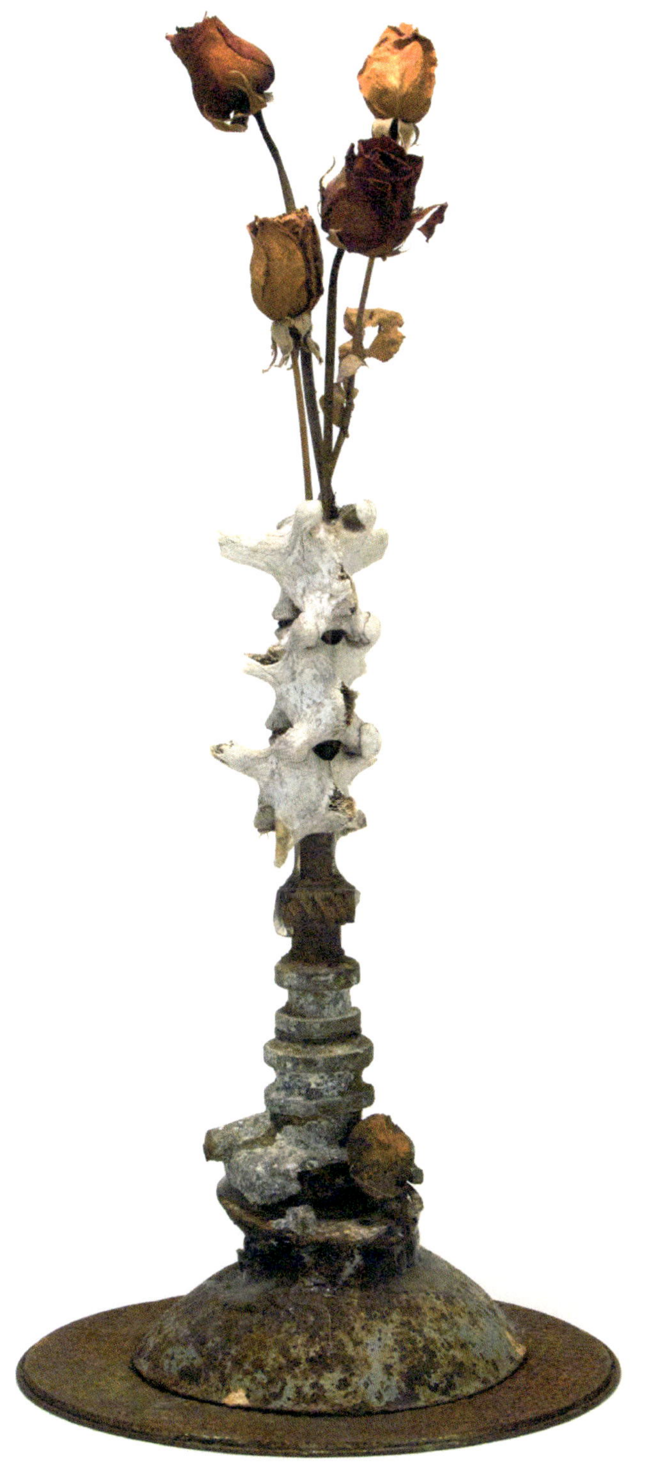



"**Urban Flowers**" • found objects from the same location • 6"x 20" • 2007

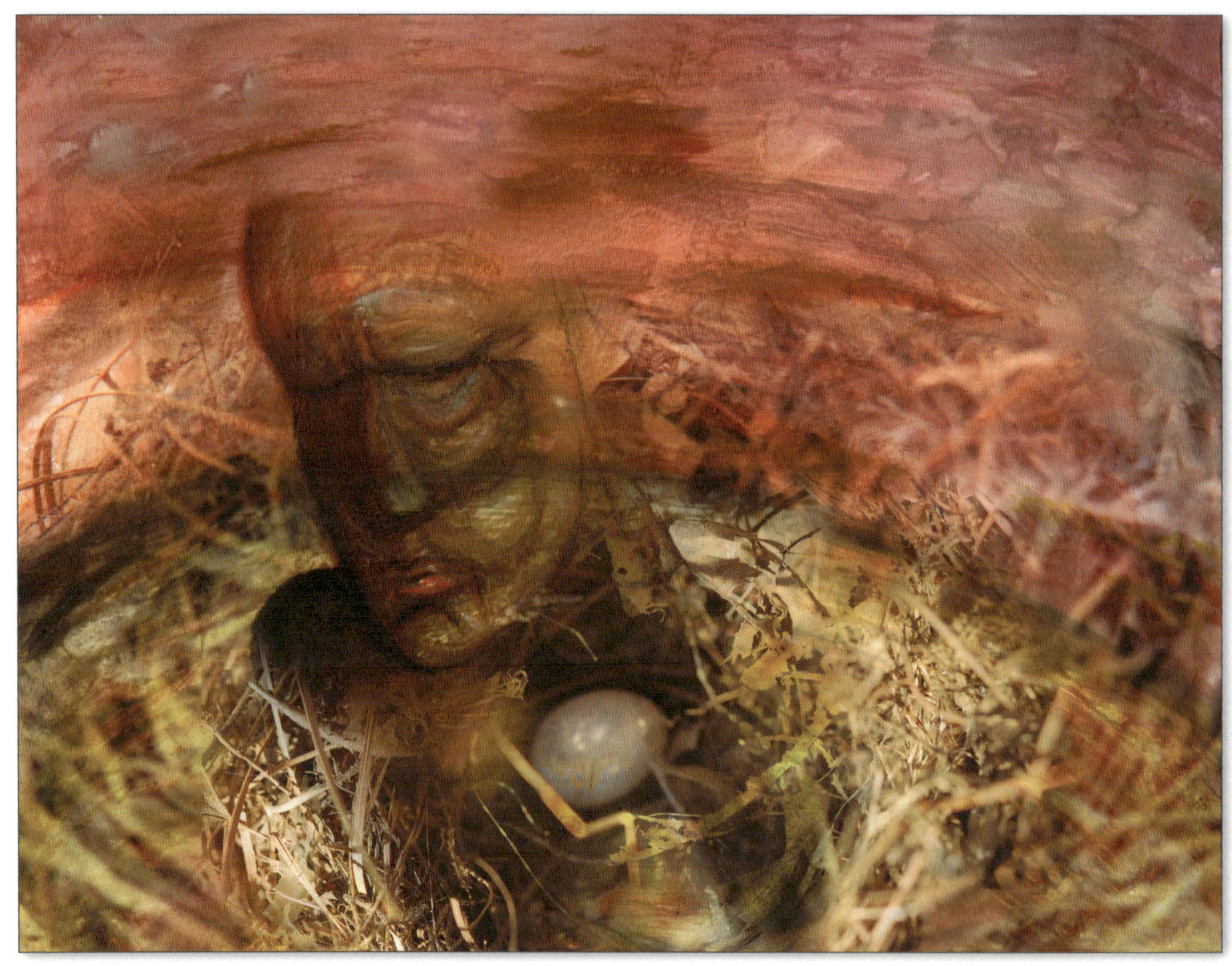

"**The Nest**" • Digital collage, ballpoint pen and pencil on watercolor paper  • 13"x 19" • 2011

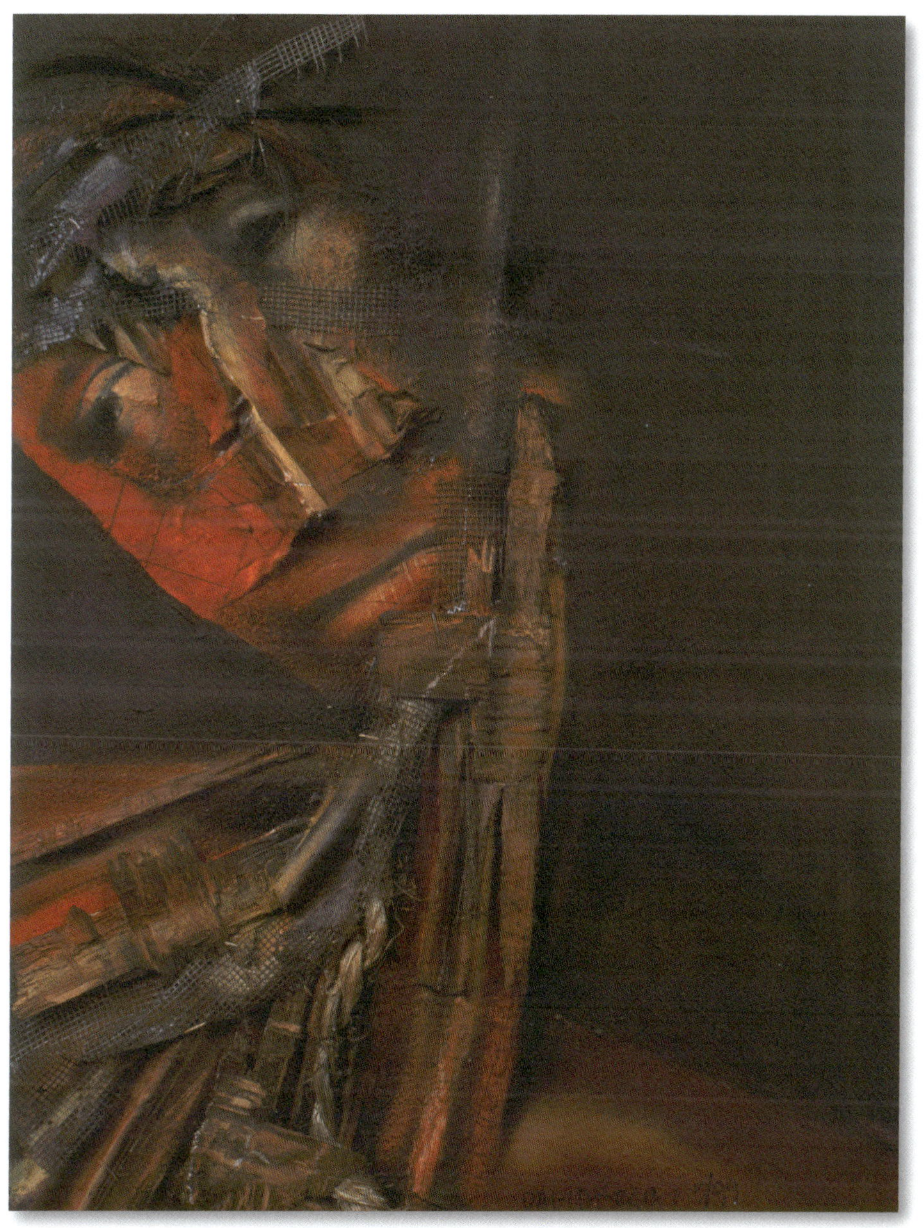



"**Surfaces No. 6**" • Oil and found objects on paper and board • 9"x 12" • 1999

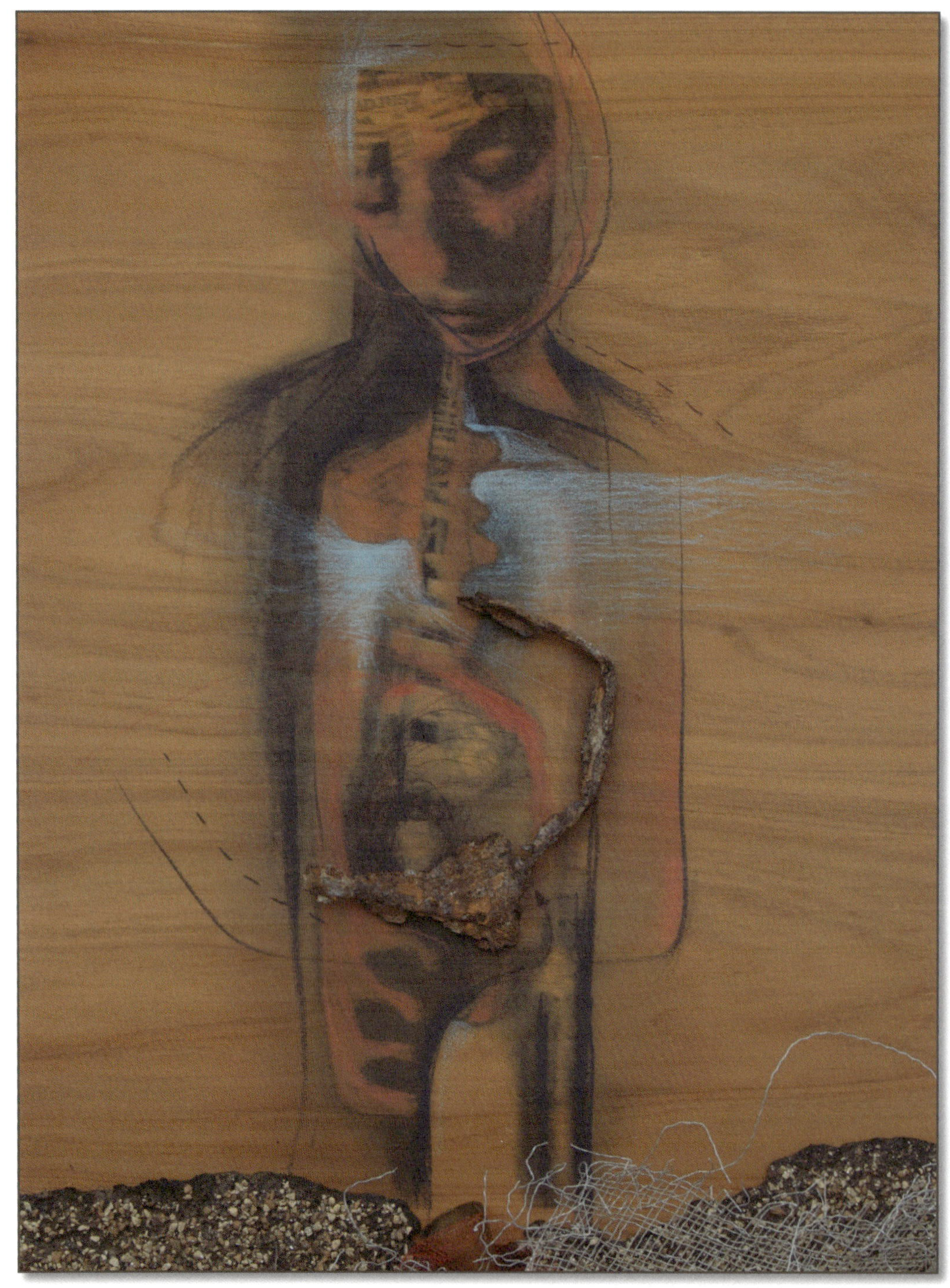

"**Adjustments**" • collage with pencil and found objects on board • 9"x12" • 2003

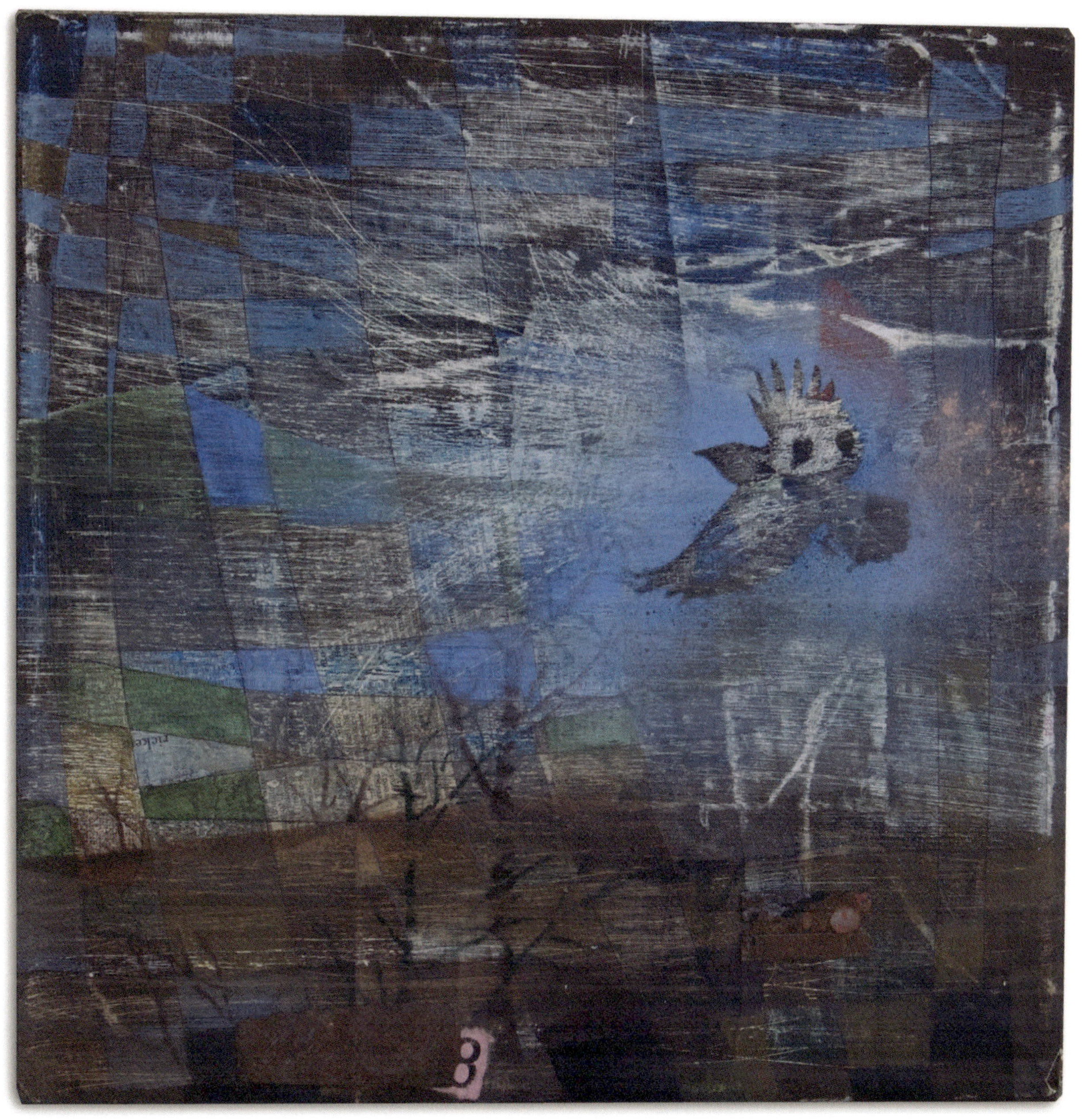

"**Dreams of Flight**" • Oil, ballpoint pen and paper on canvas • 12"x12" • 2011

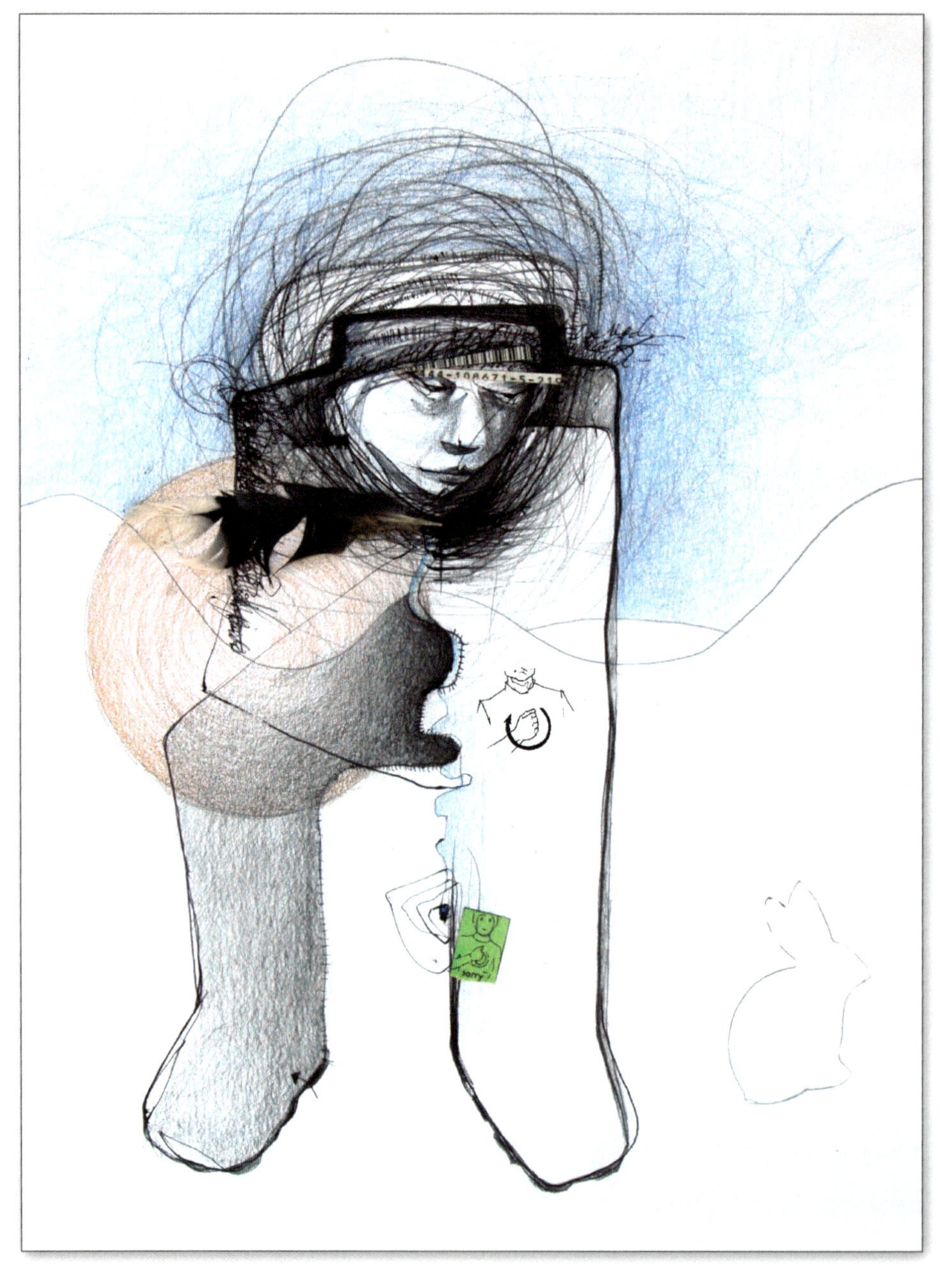



"I'm Sorry" • Ballpoint pen and collage on paper   • 8"x 10" • 2006

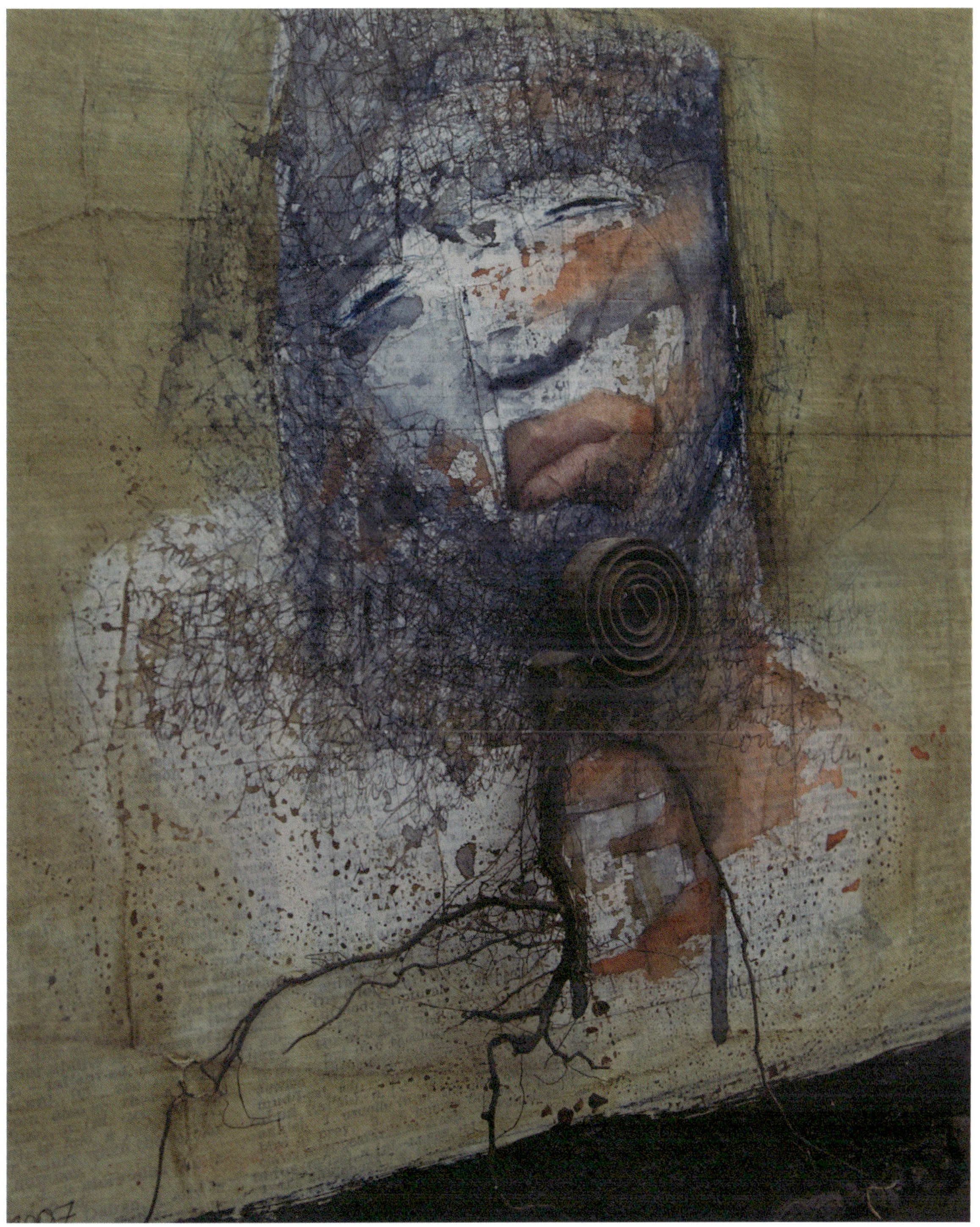

**"Uprooted"** (detail view) • Oil, ballpoint pen and paper with found objects on canvas • 13"x 13" • 2007

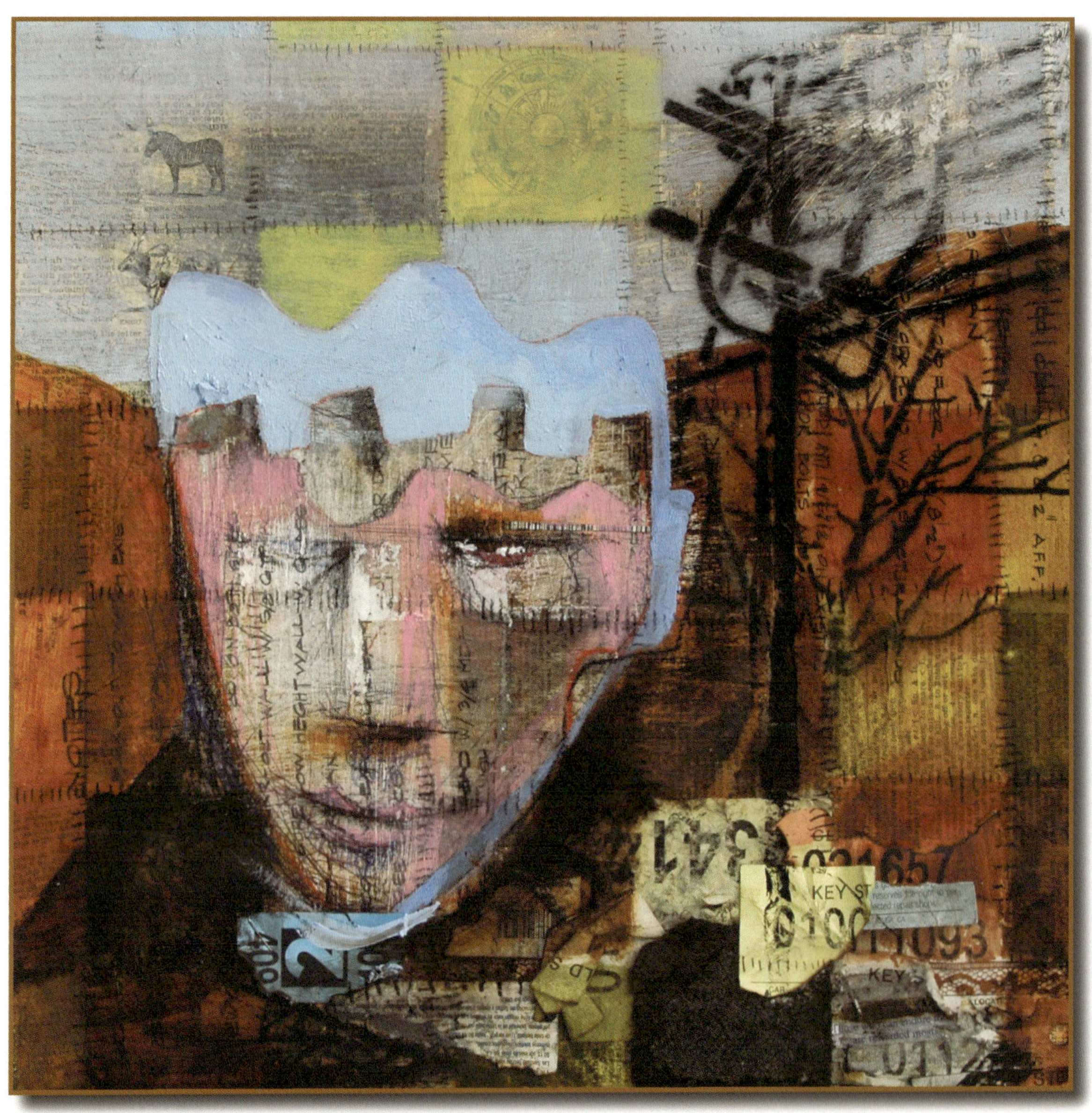

**"Portrait of Pico"** • Oil, ballpoint pen and found paper on canvas • 13"x 13" • 2009

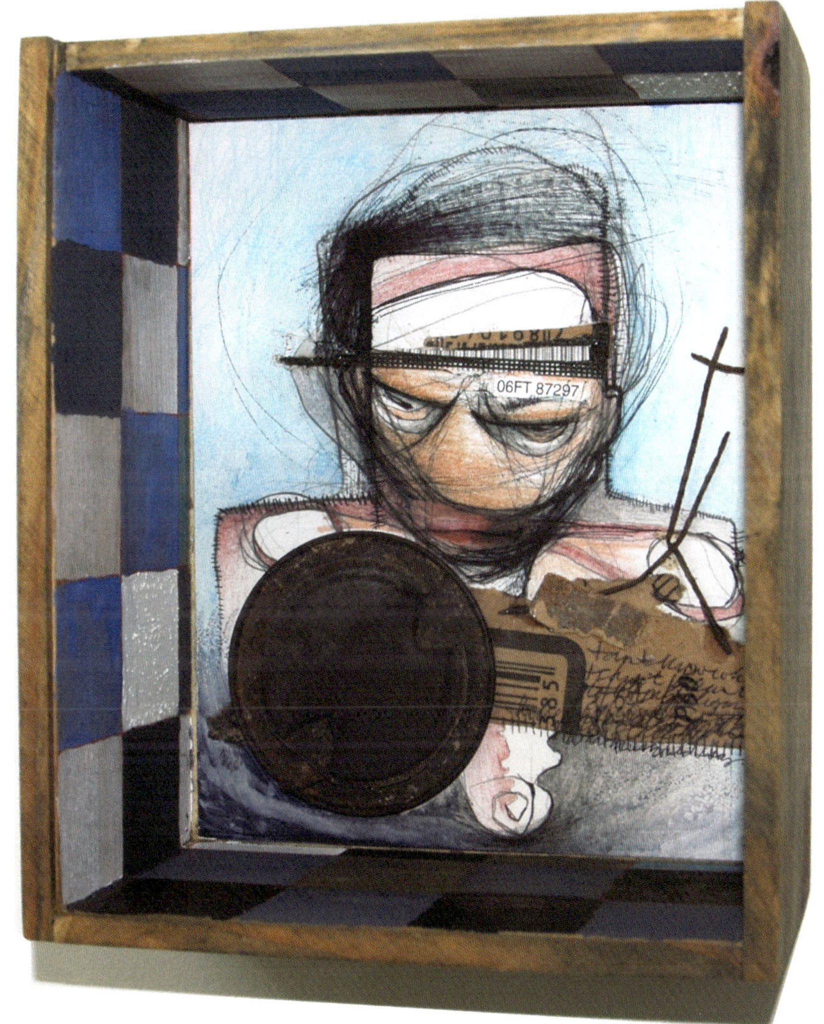



**"Defense Box"** • Oil, ballpoint pen, found objects on wood box • 8"x 9 x 8" • 2005

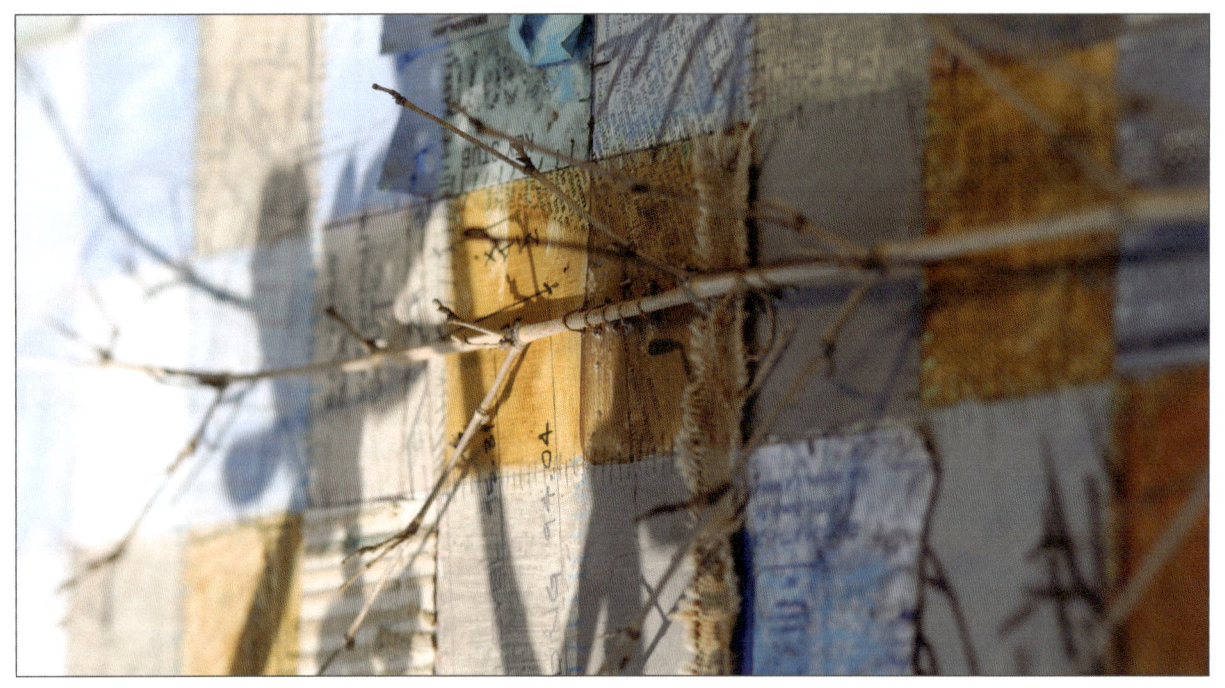

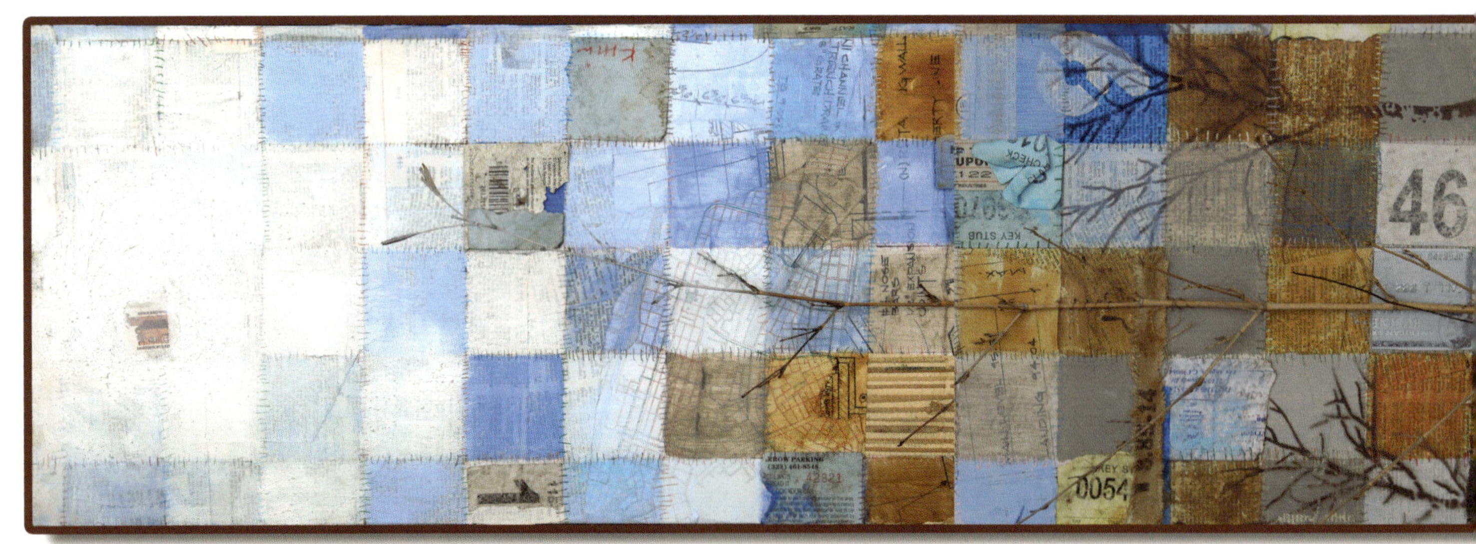

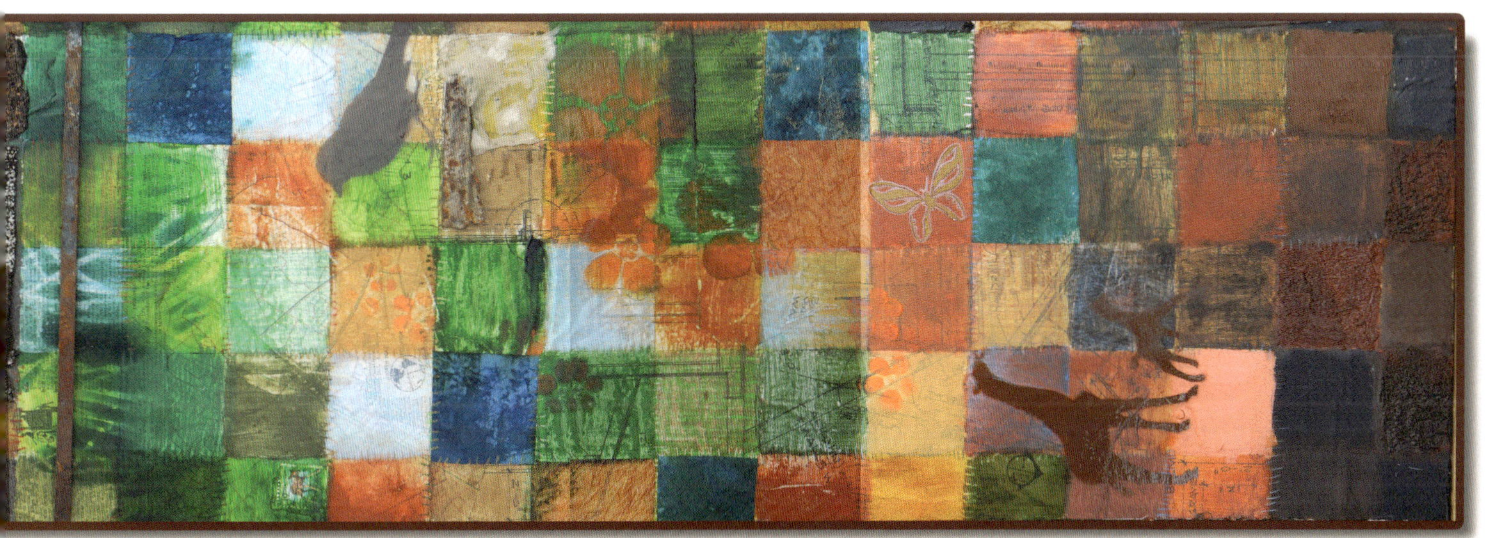

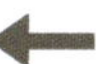

"**The End of Eden**" (horizonal view)• Oil, pencil and fabric with found objects on canvas, 11"x 61" • 2009

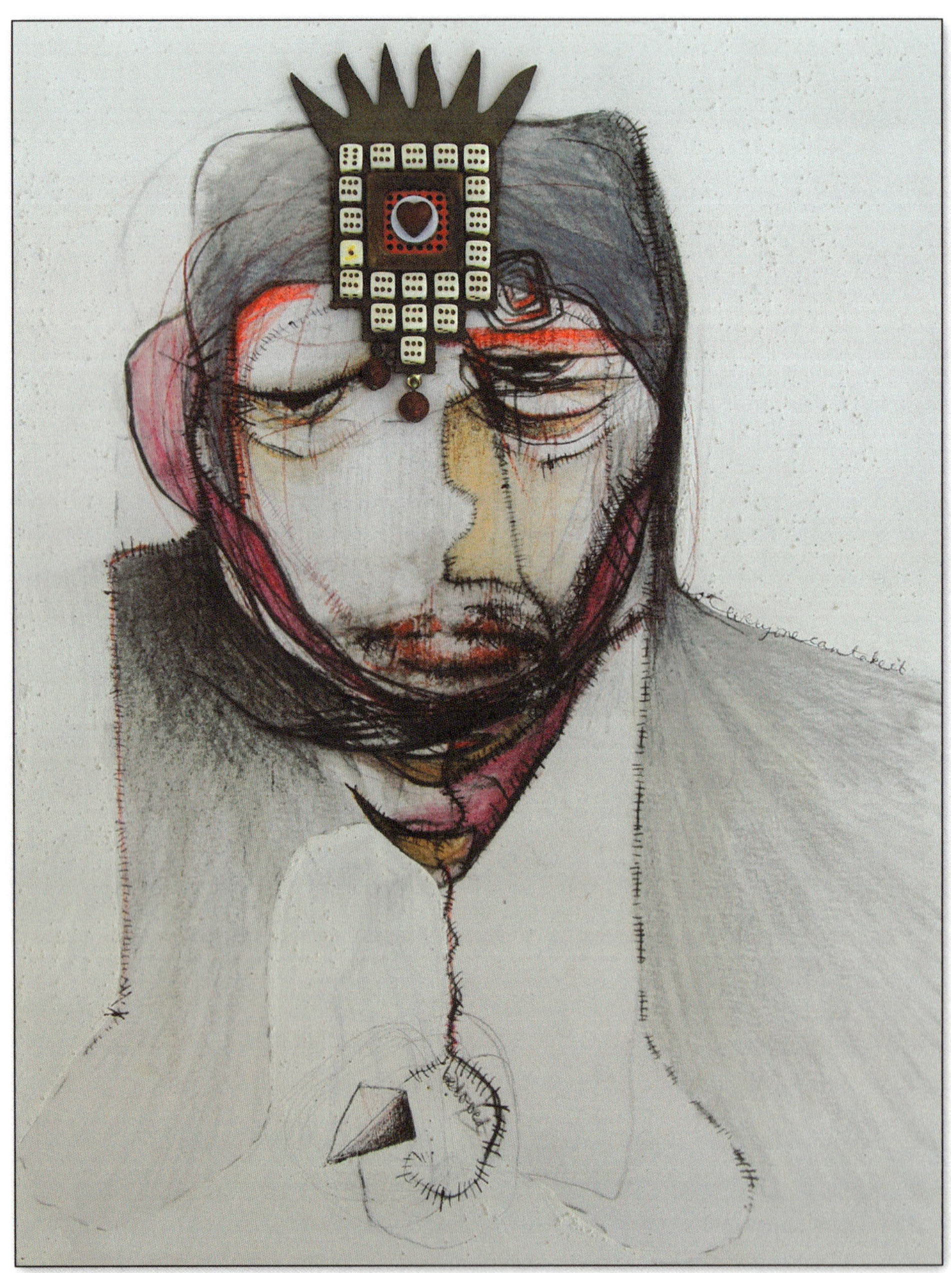

**"King David"** • Pencil with found objects on board • 9"x 12" • 2007

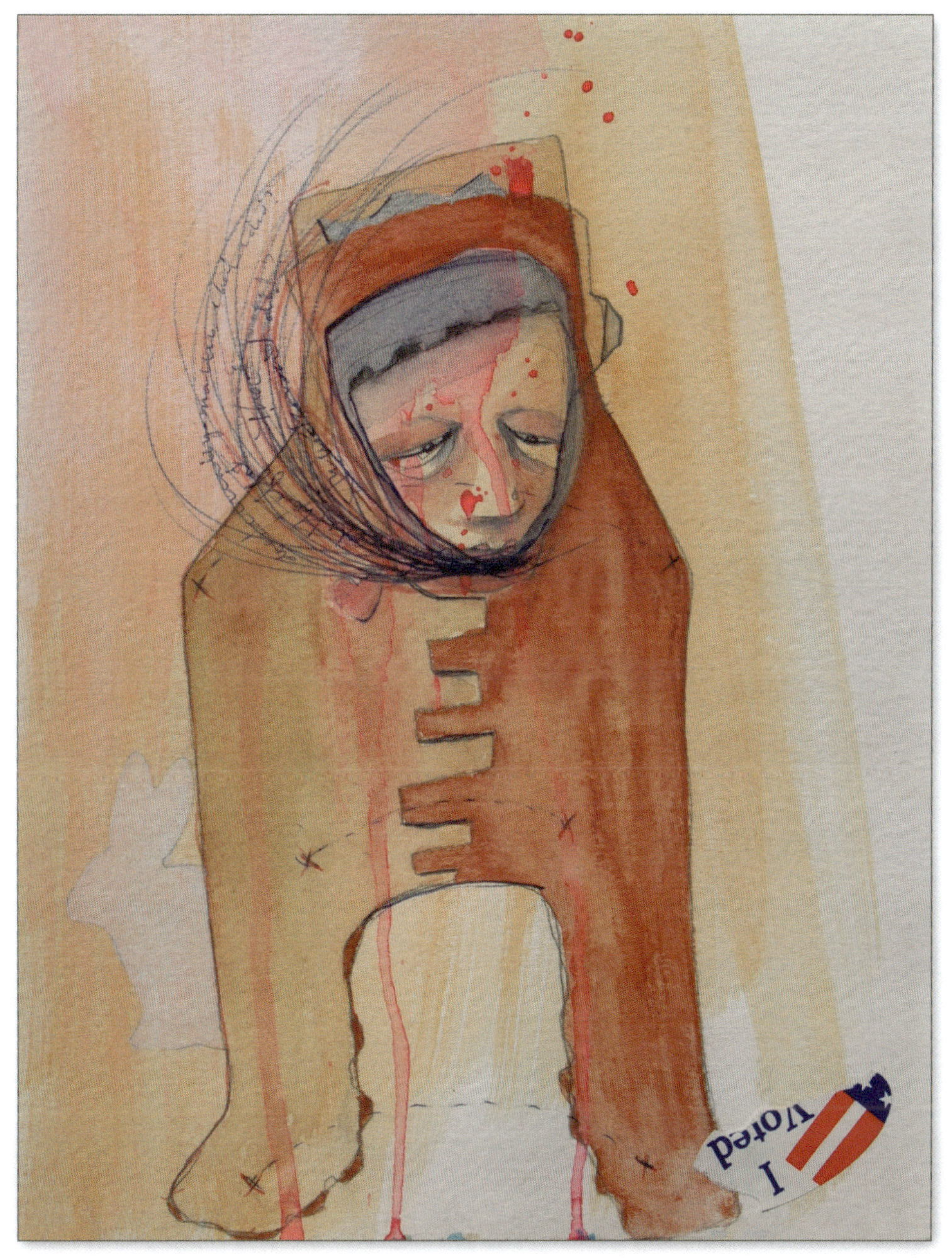



**"I Voted"** • Watercolor, ballpoint pen and sticker on board • 8″ x 10″ • 2008

CPSIA information can be obtained at www.ICGtesting.com
Printed in the USA
LVIW01n2333190917
549346LV00002B/12